T0312578

Alain Bergala

The Cinema Hypothesis:
Teaching Cinema in the Classroom
and Beyond

Translated from the French by Madeline Whittle

Österreichisches Filmmuseum
SYNEMA – Gesellschaft für Film und Medien

A book by SYNEMA ☰ Publikationen
Alain Bergala. The Cinema Hypothesis
Volume 28 of FilmmuseumSynemaPublikationen

This book was published in collaboration with the British Film Institute, Scottish Film Education, and Creative Scotland.

SYNEMA – Gesellschaft für Film und Medien
Neubaugasse 36/1/1/1, A-1070 Wien

Design and layout: Gabi Adébisi-Schuster, Wien
Copy editors: Alejandro Bachmann, Alexander Horwath
Cover photo: The 400 Blows (1959, François Truffaut)
Printed by: REMAprint
Printed and published in Vienna, Austria.
Printed on paper certified in accordance with the rules of the Forest Stewardship Council.

ISBN 978-3-901644-67-2

Österreichisches Filmmuseum (Austrian Film Museum) and SYNEMA – Gesellschaft für Film & Medien
are supported by Bundeskanzleramt Österreich / Kunst und Kultur – Abt. (II/3) Film and by Kulturabteilung der Stadt Wien.

BUNDESKANZLERAMT ▪ ÖSTERREICH

Table of Contents

INTRODUCTION
Film Education and Film Curatorship 5

Acknowledgements 10

I. THE EXPERIENCE HAS BEEN REWARDING 11

II. THE HYPOTHESIS 21

III. STATE OF THINGS, STATES OF MIND 25

IV. CINEMA IN CHILDHOOD 36

V. ONE HUNDRED FILMS FOR AN ALTERNATIVE CULTURE 53

VI. TOWARD A PEDAGOGY OF FRAGMENTS: EXCERPTS IN CONVERSATION 65

VII. TOWARD A "CREATIVE ANALYSIS" 73

VIII. CREATING IN THE CLASSROOM: STEPPING INTO CREATIVE PRACTICE 95

ALEJANDRO BACHMANN IN CONVERSATION WITH ALAIN BERGALA
"To Talk and Write about Films and to Teach Cinema are the Last
and Only Forms of Resistance Against Consumption and Amnesia" 119

Film Education and Film Curatorship

The Cinema Hypothesis *and some of its Echoes*

Great art in cinema, Alain Bergala says, can be found "each time that emotion and thought are born out of a form, a rhythm, that could not have existed but for cinema." Later, he adds: "All education must be adapted to the children and the young people to whom it is directed, but never to the detriment of its goal. If it does not respect its subject matter, if it excessively simplifies or caricatures it, even with the best pedagogical intentions in the world, it will be doing a bad job."

We still vividly remember our joy, relief, and gratitude upon reading such sentences, such a precise, yet poetic definition of art in cinema and such a principled call for a certain mode of teaching it. When *L'hypothèse cinéma* first fell into our hands, it spoke to us in ways that no other text about film education had done before. (We were lucky to have a German translation, edited by Bettina Henzler and Winfried Pauleit, since our knowledge of French would not have sufficed to fully understand in every detail what Bergala's book was suggesting.) Assuming, as we do, that cinema can play an essential part in education, the question of *how* it should find its way into the school system, remains equally essential. And here, finally, was a book that took a clear stance: its aim was to help bring cinema to schools, but also to counter the vast arsenal of bureaucratic terms and practices in which film education so often seems to be enwrapped. It avoided the widespread notion of "media literacy" as the main educational target; it didn't suggest that young people could be provided with a toolbox of standard analytical terms and methods by which all moving images could then be "decoded;" it didn't treat cinema as just another element in an endless array of audio-visual languages; and it resisted the pedagogical impulse – which is still common, at least in Europe – to frame the capacities of cinema as potentially "dangerous," as ideological instruments which can easily "seduce" the not-yet-educated person.

Bergala's effort to articulate the real educational potentials of film and to describe a very concrete – "nuts and bolts" – didactic approach is written from the perspective of someone who grew up with cinema and who perceives that art form as a lifelong companion, eagerly wanting to share and spread his passion and knowledge, but not at any price. Accordingly, *The Cinema Hypothesis* is far more than just a book on film education in schools. It is a document of a love for cinema and a sophisticated vision of its potentials for each and every individual. It is, equally, a manifesto: it asks for the medium of film to finally be integrated into an educational

5

system that has either neglected it completely or cropped it down to fit educational standards which are themselves highly disputable.

The impact that the book had on us was not only personal; it addressed our professional motivations in an institution of film curatorship that also strives to provide ongoing film education. Over the last 15 years, the Austrian Film Museum has developed a specific programme (consisting of seminars, lectures, artist workshops, screenings, and sometimes hands-on courses) for pupils ranging from 5 to 20 years old, as well as an annual teacher's training course and multiple collaborations on the university level. However, the basic tenets of this work with children and teachers derive from curatorial principles for which the Film Museum has argued since its very foundation in 1964, many of which we found echoed in Bergala's text.

For the museum's founders Peter Konlechner and Peter Kubelka, the conviction that an interested public has the right to encounter the works of cinema in as unadulterated a form as possible led to the designation of the screening space as the primary museum space; it also meant that the museum's educational work would not start with spoken introductions, books, and reading lists but by activating the cinema machine itself: illuminating a strip of celluloid by means of a projector in a dark auditorium – thus meeting at least halfway Bergala's claim as to how art education in general should work: "You might say, along these lines, that art cannot be taught, but must be encountered, experienced, transmitted by other

means than the discourse of mere knowledge, and even sometimes without any discourse at all." The first step in any form of teaching cinema is to show films, to project them in a space that was made for just that. Such a statement appears to be self-evident, but when talking to students and teachers of film we often wonder how much of their work is actually devoted to watching films in their entirety – compared to the amount of theory that is being read, discussed, and considered as essential for any "knowledge of cinema."

Another echo is sounded by the idea of the *passeur,* a term that Bergala borrows from Serge Daney and places at center stage: the "ferryman," the agent of transmission. "Guided by the lessons of their cinematic childhood," these individuals hand down their own education in cinema in the form of a passionate "initiation." The founders of the Film Museum didn't have that term yet, but they fully acted in its spirit when making choices about programming, seminars, and master classes to be conducted, and even collection-related issues: "The only possible attitude, on the part of teachers, is to talk about the films they love with total honesty – with the child within themselves – on the condition that they had themselves taken a real pleasure in viewing the films, and had not merely grasped at the adulterated pleasures of a paternalistic pedagogism according to which 'this is good for you, even if it is not good for me.'" Often, this stance also entails resistance against certain curatorial and educational practices which are viewed by politicians and cultural managers as the most "reasonable" or "audience-friendly" – and which are held up as the kind of common-sense model to which most actors in the field apparently agree. (These practices are also the ones most likely to be rewarded with smooth relations to subsidy-giving bodies and corporate sponsors.) To be a *passeur* means to trust one's own passions and biographical experiences, to put faith in their ability to impact others with a certain force, creating an excitement for cinema on a level that no marketing-based activity could ever achieve.

Again, one might think this is a self-evident statement. And again, if we let our gaze wander we can see how many institutions today – in the museum world as well as in education – are run by people with an impressive understanding of economic processes and marketing concepts but hardly any passion for the art form that (one would assume) originally led them to choose this career. Try to have an exciting, thought-provoking discussion about your shared discipline with such cultural managers and the importance of the *passeur* concept for our contemporary cultural and educational arenas becomes obvious.

What can develop from this premise is a living, breathing culture of cinema, a vibrant sphere with more than enough self-confidence regarding its future. One of its characteristics will always be its openness towards the widest possible range of aesthetic and historical choices in cinema – and in the other arts. It will try to keep as many watergates open as possible in order to allow for the "pleasure of connection," as Bergala calls it. From the viewpoint of film curatorship and film museums, this means,

for instance, avoiding the common narrowing-down of cinema to its "feature-length narrative" application, and understanding film history as something that includes both the most current and many seemingly para- or non-cinematic works and forms. A regular visitor should be enabled to develop a memory consisting of everything she or he has seen, a rhizomatic network of connections – what Bergala calls "cultural knowledge." For him this becomes a didactic tool when he relates works of film to each other by juxtaposing excerpts from all corners of the medium's history in an educational context: "This ability opens up the pleasure of finding one's way in the fraught network of artworks as they appear before us, most often in disarray, and of understanding how every work of art is inhabited by what preceded it, and by its contemporaries, in the art from which it emerged, and in the neighboring arts, even when its author knew nothing of them or rejected them outright." In teaching film, as well as in film programming and curatorship, what needs to be established is a frame of reference that strives to be as large as the medium's history itself. "This should not prevent a person from experiencing pleasure 'full-stop,' but the pleasure of connection gives us access to something more universal than the fleeting satisfaction of our own little me, here and now." Understanding literature means reading and speaking of more than just the 19th century novel, relating this specific part of its history to poetry and drama, making connections between David Foster Wallace's *Infinite Jest* and Kurt Schwitters' *The Onion* or Walt Whitman's

Leaves of Grass, or both. In a similar sense, the effort to teach, learn, show, and understand cinema must allow for connections to be made, for instance, between the first films by the Lumières, James Benning's *RR*, Keaton's *The General*, and Tony Scott's *Unstoppable.*

Last but not least, *The Cinema Hypothesis* also argues that an understanding of and education in cinema entails a heightened sensibility for the characteristics of various moving image media, and for the differences between them. A good example is Bergala's description of the DVD and its didactic potentials: "The DVD, which [around the year 2000] was beginning to be imposed as the mainstream market standard, entailed new relationships with film." The ease and speed of access that it allowed, with chapter selection and 'bonus materials,' changed "the relationship with movie-watching that one can have at home. The VHS was made mainly for watching or re-watching a film at home, as if the film were being shown on television, with the added ability to select one's own programming, set one's own schedule, and interrupt at will the playing of the film to take a break, before resuming the show. The DVD facilitated a different desire, very nearly constituting a new practice of spectatorship: that of watching a 'fragment' of a film, whichever piece you want to watch on that particular evening, and perhaps a different one tomorrow; or, indeed, of viewing such-and-such a scene from the beginning of the film, and then, immediately afterward, viewing a scene that occurs forty minutes later in the film's actual runtime. Cinephiles have al-

ways been fetishistic about film, while the DVD enables everyone to get a taste of fetishism about film 'fragments'."

There is none of the marketing rhetoric here which permeates most debates about digital media and their perceived superiority over analogue film. When he talks about the possibilities of the DVD, Bergala is interested in how it differs from the options of cinema, how it creates different viewers and a different experience of encountering films. In our own practice of exhibiting and disseminating cinema, a comparable approach has proven very successful. The exhibition programmes and archival work of the Austrian Film Museum have always (and somewhat "famously," in this day and age) focused on preserving and showing the works of film history in the medium of their original distribution; at the same time, the museum has engaged in other forms of dissemination (such as DVDs and online publications) with the express argument that these facsimiles – as long as their function as a "catalogue format" is kept transparent – enable other productive kinds of interaction with the works in question. Accordingly, when teaching film to young people in our cinema space we always show a work in its original format when the aim is to experience the film, to understand not only its semantic qualities, but its rhythms, forms, colours, and temporal qualities. When going into detail, looking at the construction of a sequence, the composition of a frame, or the relationship between two frames, the digital medium is often better suited to the task at hand – even though it is advisable to keep the basic material elements of the analogue original nearby. To an older generation, such differences (between the varying forms of moving image creation and reception) might seem very obvious, but to young people they are already partly lost, which is why it seems important to us to make them explicit and visible.

The goal to teach an understanding of cinema in all its facets is obviously helped if the educational institution in question is also a place of film curatorship: it can directly demonstrate the "working system" of cinema in its historical variants. This is a privilege that film education in school spaces mostly has to do without, a point that is also addressed in the conversation with Alain Bergala at the end of the book. Conversely, the school offers a unique terrain for film and the other arts to work their magic in a most democratic as well as highly regulated forum, by introducing intense experiences of otherness: "I still believe that art, if brought to school under the right circumstances, can change the school itself as well as those who work within it."

~

Many people try to be *passeurs* in the best sense of the word, using their personal experience and the potentials of "learning by contagion" to hand down a deep love of cinema to the next generation. Such individuals are seldom to be found among those in power, the decision-makers in the political and bureaucratic spheres, who, consciously or not, shape the future of an art form as strongly as its creators and *passeurs* – especially in regard to its potential role in public education. In France, 15 years ago, the collaboration between a passionate

politician, Jack Lang, and a passionate cinephile, Alain Bergala, enabled the nationwide implementation of a new concept of film education. One certainly wishes for this rare constellation to appear again and again, but the book at hand also invites each and every participant in the processes of film education to consider on a personal level the "political" implications of their teaching choices. The aim of empowering today's pupils to transmit the forces of cinema into the future depends on the educator's own awareness of – and respect for – its specifics and potentials as an art form.

For now, we are grateful for the opportunity to make a small contribution towards such future constellations by publishing, for the first time in English, Alain Bergala's book on the matter. We want to thank him for his ideas and active participation in the project. Our deep gratitude also goes to Mark Reid, who originally approached us with the suggestion to publish this book, to the BFI and Scottish Film Education for their help in financing it, to Madeline Whittle for her precise and inspired translation, to Ian Wall and Ted Fendt for their suggestions and to Katharina Müller for translating the conversation with Alain Bergala at the end of the book. It is dedicated to all those who teach, and teach cinema, with the conviction that "only desire instructs", all the while looking for something "more universal than the fleeting satisfaction of our own little me, here and now."

Alejandro Bachmann & Alexander Horwath,
Austrian Film Museum

ACKNOWLEDGEMENTS

I wish to thank all the people who have given me the opportunity to write on this subject in recent years (*Les enfants de cinéma*; *Le Cinéma, cent ans de jeunesse*; *Les dossiers de ingénierie educative*; *Les ailes du désir*; etc.) and all the people who have published interviews that allowed me to hone certain ideas.

I am especially grateful to Nathalie Bourgeois, to whom this cinema hypothesis owes much, thanks to her innovative pedagogical work at the Cinémathèque française; Anne Huet and Claudine Paquot, who is no longer with us but enthusiastically took the ball and ran with it.

For this edition of the book I would also like to thank Mark Reid of the British Film Institute, and the Austrian Film Museum. I am especially grateful to Alejandro Bachmann for the rigorous and warm-hearted labour he put into the actualization of this text.

DEDICATION

For Serge Daney, Philippe Arnaud, and Alain Philippon, who, as lifelong *passeurs*, have always been guided by the lessons of their cinematic childhoods.

Alain Bergala

I

The Experience Has Been Rewarding

I consider it to be a stroke of good fortune, which comes along quite rarely in one's life, to be offered the chance, one day, to implement one's ideas, which stem from more than twenty years of reflection, experience, and dialogue in a domain as thankless as teaching, where everyone, always, must start over from square one, and where the benefits of experience generally pay off rather poorly, especially in a minor field like cinema studies. When Jack Lang, in June 2000, invited me to join a small group of advisers who would be organizing a project (now known as "The Mission")[1] promoting arts education and cultural initiatives in the national ministry of education, my first instinct was to refuse, believing that this kind of position would require political and diplomatic skills that I have never possessed. When, in the end, I accepted, it was only because I yielded to the arguments of all the friends I consulted, who told me at the time that I didn't have the right to equivocate, since for once, policymak-

ers were appealing to, and placing their trust in, someone who was not a member of the inner circle of ministry personnel, but who contributed merely the value of his experience and expertise in the affected field. The resulting two years of work enabled me to gauge the difficulty involved in transforming ideas and beliefs in the real world. I dealt with all the forces of inertia, both within and outside the institution, people who quietly work against any movement, without raising any real disputation of ideas or alternative proposals, but merely because they feel immediately threatened by any change. These were the most discouraging individuals to work with, because they were impossible to convince. Fortunately, these two years also gave me the reassurance of feeling supported, in making often radical choices, by a man of conviction, who was animated for his part by an unshakeable drive to stir things up in the domain of art in schools, on the basis of a hypothesis, strong and utterly innovative in the realm of national education. Jack Lang is not a man who is easy to convince: he's capable of holding out for a long time against an idea, for as long as he does not deeply feel its legitimacy, but as soon as he deems the idea fair and justified, his support is total; he is the first to encourage its implemen-

1 "The Mission for Arts Education and Cultural Initiatives," created by Claude Mollard and directed by Jean-François Chaintreau, was established to implement, at the heart of the national ministry of Education, the policy defined in the Five-Year Plan for the development of arts and culture in schools, jointly announced on 14 December, 2000, by the two ministers of Culture and Education, Catherine Tasca and Jack Lang.

tation and to await with faithfulness and vigilance its first effects in reality. The other sizable encouragement was in the response from educators to this ministerial proposal that, after all, could have been revealed to address an imagined, rather than a real, need. These responses were proof that a large number of teachers had only been awaiting this ministerial impetus to take charge in changing, in some small way, the methodology of their profession, by opening their classrooms to this radically "different" element, the arts, and by opening themselves to another means of being present in the teacher-student relationship: engaging in a dialogue with their students.

But ultimately, as far as I'm concerned, I feel I've found the energy to undertake this "cinema project" for the sake of the children above all, who today must be very nearly in the situation in which I found myself as a child: as non-inheritors, at a distance from culture, awaiting an improbable greeting, with no great social opportunities to get by without schooling and some elective interest to which they might cling. I was immediately moved, upon viewing the earliest films of Kiarostami, by the way in which his little protagonists fixate on an object, an obsession, in order to save themselves in a world where their only chance at existence is resistance, starting with a personal passion.

All of those for whom cinema has been important in life, not as a simple pastime but as an essential element of their constitution, and who knew very early on that they would dedicate their lives, in one way or another, to this art – these individuals all hold in their heads an imaginary autobiography, a cinematic version of their life. Personally, in my own novelistic narrative, I was saved twice: by schooling and by cinema.

First, school saved me from my small-town destiny, a life in which I might never have had access to the adult life and culture that I would later embrace. Like in a Bergman film where the character, in retreat, invisible, watches a scene where life is overturned, I was present for a discussion between my mother and a primary school teacher who was in the process of persuading her that I ought to "advance to the sixth grade." Without that teacher, my horizons would have been limited for the rest of my life. The good old school of the Republic then allowed me to be independent of my parents when I enrolled as a boarder, in my sophomore year, in a teacher training college, then, thanks to IPES, to pursue university studies.

Cinema entered my life, at the heart of a sad and anxious childhood, like a lifeline which I knew, from very early on, would be my salvation. Nothing and no one pointed me to it, I didn't share it with anyone whatsoever (neither any adult nor any child my own age), but I clung to it as you would to a life preserver – even when I had the feeling I lacked all of the keys that could have ever given me access to this universe, which I had doubtless chosen as the most distant escape from my conditions of existence, and the most inaccessible. As luck would have it, in my childhood hometown there were three movie theaters (*Le Rex* and *Le Palace* on the main square, and *L'Eden* a bit farther out, across from the bus station, where they showed the big American movies), and my family situation made it possible for me to go alone, each Sunday afternoon, with total freedom, to see a film of my choosing, about which I kept absolutely silent. It was there, watching the crossing of the Red Sea in Cecil B. DeMille's *Ten Commandments*, that I was seized by the certainty that cinema was important to me, and would be important to me from that point on, for my whole life. This private revelation would necessarily lead me much later towards a cinema that is as different as can be from the grandiloquence of that biblical Hollywood imagery: the cinema of Rossellini or Godard. I discovered only a few years ago, in gathering the texts for the book *Cet enfant de cinéma que nous avons été*,[2] that this very film, by which I naturally believed myself to be the only person ever to have been miraculously moved, had played an identical role as the "big bang" for other little boys of my generation, who had also taken it as their imaginary point of departure toward the continent of cinema. Looking back, it seems clear to me today that this "elective" interest in cinema as "my own" fiercely guarded object, not to be shared, was a way of refusing what my father was trying to pass on

to me (all of which was contrary to cinema, and more in line with hunting, poaching, life in the woods), and of choosing for myself what would save me.

Then came the much hoped-for period of my studies in Aix-en-Provence, the first truly happy time in my life, after years of roaming in the Var with my mother during childhood and my exile in boarding school during adolescence. While there, I devoted much more time to my cinephilia than to my academic studies. Each year I saw more than 300 films there, and I started to organize evening gatherings at the local Ciné-club, which possessed a very rich film collection. This was the period in which the love of cinema morphed into a desire and a need to have seen every film, which in turn developed into a proselyte's drive to convey this passion to others. I shared my cinephilia, for the first time, with a small group of diehards, loving cinema above all else, using as a touchstone everything that surrounded them, dedicating a great deal of time and energy to the group. My cinephilia had been exacerbated by the feeling that I had been in a bit of a provincial exile, whereas the Parisian cinephiles could access at will all of the films that we dreamt of seeing, as referenced in the mythic *Cahiers du cinéma*, for whose unpredictable arrival we would be on the lookout each month, scanning the shelves of a bookstore in Cours Mirabeau. It was in the course of this student life that I was introduced, belatedly, to the first of my *passeurs*[3] in Aix-en-Provence, in the person of Henri Agel, who taught there at the time: the number of individuals whose voca-

---

2 *Cet enfant du cinéma que nous avons été* (That Child of Cinema We Have Been), Institut de l'Image d'Aix-en-Provence, 1993.

3 Editor's note: The French term *passeur* describes a ferryman who smuggles goods from one shore to the other, but can also refer to someone who relays or passes a ball to the next person in line. Bergala uses it throughout in the context of cinephilia, in reference to the critic Serge Daney, who spoke of the critic as someone who passes down his love or passion for cinema to others (see also footnote 16).

tions he sparked or bolstered is well-known. There were training courses organized by the federations of Ciné-clubs that were flourishing in this period, like the famous clubs of Pézenas or Marly-le-Roi, where I met Jean Douchet for the first time during a retrospective of thirty or so films by John Ford, whose credits were strung together in chronological order like in a dream, during a week where, cut off from the world, we saw John Wayne age from film to film and become more and more magnetic while giving less and less of a damn. It was at the Rencontres d'Avignon where, very intimidated, I crossed paths for the first time with the editors of Cahiers du cinéma, who seemed to me to belong to an inaccessible caste. Pascal Bonitzer was the one whose "edge" terrified me the most. I was still far from imagining that one day I would have the audacity to write in that journal, alongside these personalities who were, to my eyes, so prestigious.

Subsequently, I taught for two years in Morocco, where I had the good fortune of meeting Roland Barthes; upon my return to Paris, he led me to Christian Metz's seminar, where I would remain for years without ever completing my degree, staying as much out of admiration for his humanity as a teacher as for the actual content of his teaching. It was also during my difficult come-down in Paris, where I had never lived before, when Ignacio Ramonet – who had also just returned from Morocco – invited me to write my first articles for the movie page of Le Monde Diplomatique, for which he had recently assumed responsibility.

I was thereafter obliged to divide my professional life between writing and editing for Cahiers du cinéma (where Jean-Louis Comolli helped me come in through the back door, during the journal's terrible Maoist period), directing films (thus realizing what were, for me, the most shameful dreams of the child I had been: to shoot feature-length fiction films), and teaching cinema. I experienced varying degrees of tension and happiness in moving between these three activities, all of which were vital to my stability and my instability alike.

The third route, my work in film education, began with a foundational pedagogical experience at CEC de Yerres,[4] where I managed to have some success, over the course of two years, in developing an introductory curriculum in cinema studies for classes of seventh- and eighth-graders – working in a setting that offered true-to-life resources, under nearly ideal conditions and with a team of enthusiastic teachers. I created a primary toolbox designed to cultivate the elements of cinematic narrative, in the form of games involving film

4 The Center of Education and Culture (Centre éducatif et culturel) in the Yerres valley was an experimental site established in 1968, an "integrated center" whose aim, put forward by Malraux, was to bring together in a single architectural ensemble a college and cultural, athletic, and socio-educational facilities, which would work together in concert. The experiment that I was able to lead there, coming from the Center for Cultural Initiatives (Centre d'Action Culturelle), in the direction of Guillaume Budé College, was the subject of two publications: Pour une pédagogie de l'audio-visuel (éditions de La Ligue de l'enseignement, 1975), and Initiation à la sémiologie du récit en images (éditions de La Ligue de l'enseignement, 1977).

slides, a tool whose lack I have felt in my own pedagogical practice, and which was shown, at the time, to fulfill a general need, meriting large-scale circulation and a great many users scattered across France. Some of those users still speak of it with nostalgia, more than twenty years later.

This experience in Yerres opened another door for me, this time at the university where I worked as a teaching fellow: Michel Marie invited me to design a curriculum around the question of cinema studies pedagogy at Paris III, where I was to return two decades later, after a long detour through the universities of Lyon 2 and Rennes 2. Teaching cinema in universities has always represented a necessary and restorative reunion for me, to which I give myself over with real pleasure, and with a taste for helping certain students – not necessarily the "best" – to find themselves in cinema, even if it's a far cry from their original aspirations. Teaching at university level has not diminished in my estimation the mode of instruction that I have never stopped practicing, working with diverse provincial audiences at local movie theaters, in the form of seminars and other cinematic weekend retreats – which, it seems to me, have long since replaced the educational tradition of the Ciné-clubs.

In spite of this three-pronged approach to my professional activities, which should have protected me from any kind of exclusive or overly reductive "branding," I've been aware once again, during these two years spent at "The Mission," how indelible was the mark left on me by the experience of belonging to *Cahiers*, even after more than fifteen years. It's true that, to this day, I remain a loyal fellow traveler with the journal, which was the place where I learned the most, and learned of nothing but cinema, and where I felt what might have been a kind of learning by contagion, listening to Serge Daney or Jean Narboni talk interminably about films that they had just seen, even if these dialogues were never addressed directly to me, but overheard "slantwise," while I worked on something else. All the same, I naively thought that they were giving me credit, during this mission at the ministry of education, for having only ever written about films that I loved, and for having opened up the journal to a little outside air by going to film shoots to meet and interview crew members and actors – in short, for not entirely adhering to the caricature of a *Cahiers* editor, sectarian and entrenched in his armchair cinephilia. But old myths die hard. As always, affiliation with a powerful symbolic entity wins out over whatever one has actually done: Once more, this family brand has resounded in my life as a mark of distinction (for some) and of infamy (for others). For both groups, incidentally, this affiliation is as fantastical as it is real: the wife of one filmmaker even wrote to the minister to denounce me for not responding quickly enough to her letter, imputing this negligence to my "obligation" to uphold an old hatred that I had always demonstrated as a critic, with regard to her husband. Of course, the filmmaker in question was one whose films I rather like, and about whom I've never written a word.

Anyone who has worked at *Cahiers* in any lasting way, regardless of what he wrote there, is forever suspected of intellectualism and sectarian dogmatism, whether in the context of receiving government support for film production projects, or at state dinners with filmmakers whom the journal has not really championed. It's no picnic (for me, in any case) when one is supposed to assume a new role in which one must respond to questions of all kinds, arbitrate proposals, but also solicit support and collaborations. I'm grateful to Jack Lang for having entrusted me with this mission in full knowledge of the facts, without worrying that this "Cahiers" label would constitute a disadvantage for his policy goals of bringing cinema as an art into schools.

It was at this moment, around late 2000 and early 2001, that Jack Lang and Catherine Tasca launched their so-called "Five-Year Plan" to introduce the arts into schools in a manner different from before. This was also the moment and the framework in which I found myself entrusted with the task of conceiving a proposal for cinema studies – and the moment itself was not indifferent to the subject of cinema. The culture of spectatorship was in the process of changing at high speed, with the arrival of multiplexes and membership cards, and with the new mode of engaging with film that began, tentatively, to be introduced by DVD technology. The increasingly dense concentration of distribution and exhibition networks led to a state of cinematic offerings where a third of all French multiplexes were releasing the same

film on the same Wednesday, at the same fateful 2 p.m. screening time, in thousands of theaters at once, leaving the less well-supported films (lacking the advantages of commercial appeal and marketing budget) with less and less of a chance of finding their audience: the competition between two movies would sometimes be played out with 1500 prints of one film versus 3 of the other. This concentration of funding streams and synergistic film-television coproductions would have meant that French cinema, on the whole, would have done better, with ticket sales rising appreciably, but with the fast-moving threat of standardization "from above" over production, imposing a much-acclaimed, and rather effective, "success-driven model," to the detriment of "small" movies and art films. This system encourages, to general approval, big-scale national films to increasingly squash smaller films, without real remorse, in the name of French cinema's general resistance, on French territory, against the American blockbusters. Alas, in this resistance, it often becomes a question of imitating the enemy, to the point of no longer really knowing who one is oneself, as in the films of Fritz Lang (I'm thinking of *Man Hunt*) where it becomes necessary to dehumanize oneself, lose one's soul, take up the arms of the enemy in order to effectively fight him. It's true that the French system, in isolated examples (advances on ticket sales, etc.), still allows for small films to be made, though it then leaves them with practically no chance at all of surviving in theaters in any significant way. The networks of independent, art house, and experimental cinemas, which have long been the principal distribution channels for such marginalized films, were beginning to take the measure of these changes and of the increasing difficulty that they would face thenceforth to maintain the public's interest and curiosity with regard to an art cinema doomed to survive under these new conditions.

Cinema's technical parameters were also undergoing a transformation, with the increasingly irreversible transition from the analog to the digital. Two phases in the life of a film are still somewhat resistant to the digital today: filming, for the majority of movies, and theatrical distribution, the only two steps in the process where the film image is still analog, inscribed in a chemical medium.[5] Even so, some films are already being shot on digital cameras in very high definition, and digital projection in theaters will come soon enough. For most people, this digital transformation translates to the arrival on the market of mini DV cameras and the first computer editing programs that now make up part of the standard arsenal of software suggested for purchase by manufacturers upon buying a new computer. The implications of this spread of the digital constitute a minor revolution in the relationship between school and cinema: for the first time in the history of education, we have at our disposal equipment that is light, ultra-easy to use, and relatively inexpensive.

5 Editor's note: At the time of the text's original French-language publication, in 2002, the use of digital technologies for filming, editing, and theatrical projection were not yet standard.

The DVD, at least, which was beginning to be imposed as the mainstream market standard, entailed new relationships with film. The ease and speed of access that the DVD allowed, with chapter selection and "bonus materials," is in the process of changing the relationship with movie-watching that one can have at home. The VHS was made mainly for watching or re-watching a film, at home, as if the film were being shown on television, with the added ability to select one's own programming, set one's own schedule, and interrupt at will the playing of the film to take a break, before resuming. The DVD facilitated a different desire, very nearly constituting a new practice of spectatorship: that of watching a "fragment" of a film, whichever piece you want to watch on that particular evening, and perhaps a different one tomorrow; or, indeed, of viewing such-and-such a scene from the beginning of the film, and then, immediately afterward, viewing a scene that occurs forty minutes later in the film's actual runtime. Cinephiles have always been fetishistic about film, while the DVD enables everyone to get a taste of fetishism about film "fragments." Film exhibitors might have worried, for a brief period, that "home cinema," as the equipment manufacturers called it, with its high technical quality (with respect to reproduction, support, and home viewing capabilities), would take moviegoing audiences out of theaters, giving them the added benefit of shortened distribution delays between theatrical and DVD release dates. Today it seems that these fears were unfounded, and that spectators who buy DVDs of a film are the same ones who had gone to see the film in theaters at the time of its release. We have long known that people who go to concerts are the same people who buy the most CDs, and that people who visit museums are the same people who buy art books. The day will come, perhaps, when you will buy a movie on DVD at the movie theater ticket counter, upon leaving the theater, so as to get a different, more personal use out of the film at home.

This moment of crisis and transformation of everything that constitutes a global culture of cinema – the viewer, the relationship between viewer and film, the technology, the economics – was the ideal moment in which to formulate a brand-new hypothesis, which would attempt to take into account everything that was in the process of changing, visibly, in the field of cinema, but also in the field of education: something has been overturned in the educational relationship that can be identified as the cutting of a cord. The good old conflict of the generations, which in fact was merely a short-lived opposition between sons and fathers as to whether the sons should be allowed to exist as a new generation, never prevented a shared and continuous culture from forming, in spite of everything, between the fathers and sons. It is obviously something different, and more serious, that for several years has been endangering educational relationships outside traditional bourgeois settings: a much more radical cord-cutting. Certain "youth" cultures (which are produced in part by the media, and in which cinema plays a decisive role in establishing a template) have been established as strong cultures, but on the basis of a rejection of narrow-minded community values, as much in opposition to the cultural values of their origins as to those circulated in schools.

When I took charge of this project, I myself was engaged in a three-pronged practice of cinema instruction, not to mention my life of domestic globetrotting through French movie theaters and seminars of all kinds. First, at the university, where I have been trying for years to lay the foundations for a mode of film analysis that would be centered around the act of creation; second, in a series entitled "School and Cinema,"[6] for which I've recently finished drafting several teaching guides on some of my favorite films (*Moonfleet* and *Where Is the Friend's Home?*, among others), and which coproduced my two cassette tapes on *Le Cinéma, une histoire de plans (Cinema, A Story in Shots)*, where I tried to apply an open, multifaceted, and lively reading of the film shot; third, and above all, at the Cinémathèque française, where since 1995 I have taken part in an experiment in avant-garde pedagogy christened "Cinema, One Hundred Years Young,"[7] which was the true laboratory and prototype, in my eyes, of what I will propose for classes in "cinema as an artistic project", or CAP classes.

6 The association *Les enfants du cinéma* (Children of Cinema), founded in 1994 by the ministers of Culture and National Education, is charged with implementing the national series *School and Cinema*.

7 *Le Cinéma, cent ans de jeunesse* (Cinema, one hundred years young) is an experimental educational series, created in 1995 and coordinated by the education department of the Cinémathèque française, and led by Nathalie Bourgeois.

Upon implementing this plan for bringing the arts into the classroom, I discovered that a government official is not guaranteed to be obeyed, even in his clearest directives, and that a concept's passage down through all of the layers and filters of the hierarchy can result in even the clearest and keenest messages being transformed upon reaching the "ground," splattering like wet cat food, you might say, if not entirely upturned. In order for an idea or a conviction to succeed in retaining even the slightest bit of its innovative character, its color, and its luminosity after having passed through all these dulling filters – as might an image caught on camera – the idea must be especially radical and focused from the start. The successive translations will have many ways of dampening its initial impact, of leading it astray, if not defacing it outright. This is one of the reasons for my desire and need to write this book: to come back – after a year and a half of quarrels (in and outside of the institution), explanations, and proselytising – to several principles that have guided this exploit, in order to reaffirm them in their original vigor after giving them a trial run in the real world, for I believe that they are still valid and that they bear a great potential for transformation. In this field as in all others, real changes take place when something in the symbolic system has been overturned first: reality always follows in the end, though it may drag its feet a little or a lot. It's here, in the symbolic order, that the real barriers and oppositions are found. From this perspective, it's not always a bad thing to "put the cart before the horse": it might be the only way, in the heavy machinery of national education, to get things moving. If you sensibly put the horse first, you run the risk that they might be too old to pull the cart when they finally reach their destination, at a time when civil society will have long since moved on to automobiles. In the realm of cinema, regardless of what the future evolution of the arts-in-schools plan might bring about, something has shifted, in the symbolic system, which has made it worth the effort, and has benefited the very idea of cinema's legitimacy as an art in the classroom. Already, productions and changes in mentality are demonstrating this.

In arts education, there are few general aims, grand and generous: to reduce inequality, to draw out other character skills in intuition and sensitivity, to develop critical minds, etc. The job of a government official is to affirm these aims steadfastly and ceaselessly. On the side of concrete pedagogical experience, there has always been the discourse among practitioners who bump up against reality every day, caught between opposition from the higher-ups and the challenges confronted in the classroom, which every teacher tries to resolve pragmatically, with a greater or lesser degree of personal and professional gratification. What's most lacking in the field of arts education is an idea that runs between the two extremes, a tactical idea that would be strengthened by conviction in the grand aims that guide it – say, the great objectives of public education, which still need defending and are on the agenda now more than ever before

– and that would be as vigilant about the challenges of actually translating these general ideas into pedagogical practice as it would be with regard to the validity of overly pragmatic discourse. If goodwill and enthusiasm do not come about by default – at least on the part of government officials and educators (the situation between the two groups is another matter) – it's clear that in education it is always very difficult to mitigate every possible slip-up that might end up corrupting the meaning of what has been undertaken, even when armed with conviction and generosity. We must question all forms of pragmatism that result in profit where there's no one left to thoroughly assess what is being done and why, especially if what's being done seems to be "working." In education more than in other fields, we must forever be wary of criteria based on "what works," which is never a sufficient validation – since, after all, globalization works, trade works, the media works, the division of labor works, demagoguery works, but are these really things we want to pass down and reproduce?

All education must be adapted to the children and the young people to whom it is directed, but never to the detriment of its goal. If it does not respect its subject matter, if it excessively simplifies or caricatures it, even with the best pedagogical intentions in the world, it will be doing a bad job. This is especially true for cinema, where children aren't expecting to be taught to "read" films, so to speak, so that they might become utterly competent, and contented, film viewers even before undergoing any instruction. The main cause for concern is often the (legitimate) fear of teachers who never received specific training in this subject area, and who cling to instructional shortcuts that offer comfort, but which betray cinema without fail. These shortcuts almost always submit to film as a meaning generator (the author chose this angle or that framing in order to signify such-and-such) or, in a less severe case, an emotion generator. What is key, I am becoming increasingly convinced, is not even the teacher's "knowledge" of cinema; it's the way in which he or she makes use of the subject: it's possible to speak very simply, and without fear, about cinema, if you only adopt the correct posture, the correct relation to the cinematic object. This is the principal ambition of this book: to convince those who want to hear it that such a goal is attainable, to help them in attaining it if they wish to do so, and to accept all the consequences, which are immense, of truly regarding cinema as an art – a step which will represent a small revolution in education, whose significance we can still just barely glimpse.

II

The Hypothesis

Jack Lang's grand hypothesis on the question of arts education was centered on an encounter with otherness.[8] We witnessed something strange: a national education official proposed bringing art into primary schools as something radically different, something that would necessarily constitute a break with the established norms of teaching and of classical pedagogy. This hypothesis had the courage to distinguish arts education from training in the arts – a distinction that did not fail to trouble educators in the traditional artistic disciplines – and to affirm the principle that art, without being stripped of an essential dimension, cannot be restricted to artistic training alone, in the traditional sense of a subject area inscribed in the curriculum and on students' schedules, entrusted to a specialist instructor, competitively recruited. The hypothesis derives its strength and its novelty from the conviction that any form of confinement within this disciplinary logic will degrade the symbolic significance of the subject matter and its revelatory power, in the photographic sense of "revelation." Art, in order to remain art, must remain a catalyst for anarchy, scandal, disorder. Art is by definition a sower of trouble within the institution. It cannot be understood by students without the experience of "doing" and without contact with the artist, the craftsperson, like a "foreign body" in the classroom, like a pleasantly disruptive element in the school's value system, its code of conduct, and its relational norms. Art must be neither the exclusive property nor the private domain of a specialist teacher. It must be an experience of a different nature, in the elementary classroom, than the one offered by a specialized course, as much for the students as for the teachers. This strong and novel idea, moreover, did not fail to provoke turmoil and opposition at the heart of the national education apparatus, at every level of the hierarchy. The institution has a natural tendency to standardize, to amortize, indeed to absorb that element of risk represented by an encounter with any form of otherness, in order to reassure itself, and to reassure its agents.

Jean-Luc Godard, in the cinematic self-portrait *JLG/JLG*, whispers: "For there is the rule, and there is the exception. There is culture, which is the rule, and there is the exception, which is art. Everyone talks about the rule – computers,

---

8 Editor's note: Bergala uses the French *"l'altérité,"* a term mostly used in philosophical and cultural theory discourses to refer to the other, or otherness, as something the individual (or a society as a whole) distinguishes itself from in order to define its own identity.

T-shirts, television – and no one talks about the exception, it's never talked about. It's written (Flaubert, Dostoevsky), it's composed (Gershwin, Mozart), it's painted (Cézanne, Vermeer), it's filmed (Antonioni, Vigo)."

You might say, along these lines, that art cannot be taught, but must be encountered, experienced, transmitted by other means than the discourse of mere knowledge, and even sometimes without any discourse at all. Teaching is concerned with the rule, while art must aspire to the rank of the exception. Jack Lang held fast to a position between his role as government official (protector of the institution and its order), and his conviction that art must remain an experience "apart" in school, through which students must rub up against its radical otherness. He fought to maintain equilibrium in this contradiction between institution and otherness – even if, in reality, the contradiction inevitably weakened the implementation and expansion of his project, insofar as the sole path to legitimization for any discipline or field, in the national ministry of education, remains a standardized curriculum and competitive recruitment process. By the same logic, Lang maintained that the initiative for leading an art class still resided in personal, voluntary engagement by educators who express a desire to engage, regardless of their discipline.

Personally, as a teacher in the university, I was intensely questioned by students of cinema studies, who considered it scandalous that their specialized course of study would not open doors for them toward a teaching profession concerned with cinema. They reacted, at the time, in the name of the coherence of the scholarly system that had formed them up to that point, where "teaching" equaled "competitive training and specialized professorship," without wondering whether it was a good thing in itself, for the art that they had chosen, to "accommodate" it, in all senses of the word, in a traditional educational model. The only honest response that one could give them was that it would perhaps be up to them to seek another means of bringing their expertise in cinema into schools, rather than becoming lifelong professors-of-cinema. Certain former cinema students, who had already bumped up a bit against the world of working in film, had been engaged in that search since the first wave of arts-oriented courses.

Finally, the one fundamental question that is truly worth the effort of raising it is the following: can an institution like the national ministry of education take art (and cinema) into account as a site of otherness? I'm obviously not referring to the administrative onerousness of an apparatus of this size and conservatism, but instead to the real paradox that this project represents for the institution. Is primary school the place for this kind of work? Is it well-placed to carry it out? An answer suggests itself: primary school, as it currently functions, is not made for such work, but at the same time, for the majority of children today, it is *the only* place where an encounter with art can take place. Thus schools are duty-bound to do this work, even at the risk of disrupting their own habits and mentalities somewhat. For most children (with the exception of "heirs," in the sense used by Bourdieu), civil society has already ceased to offer anything more than cultural commodities that are quickly consumed, quickly obsolete, and socially "mandatory." Those who oppose arts education in primary schools often turn up their noses to proclaim that everything that comes out of schools is tarnished with the fact of obligation and thus will never be suited for the arrival of the arts, which should fall within the jurisdiction of a modest individualism. They never mention the obligation to see films that's imposed on us by the big distribution networks and the bludgeoning assault of the media. If the encounter with cinema as an art does not occur in primary school, there are many children for whom there is a strong chance it will never occur anywhere. I still don't know if the national ministry of education can take art into account as a site of otherness, but I remain convinced that it must, and that, with primary schools as its starting point, it can.

This general hypothesis about art in primary schools, encouraged by the government official for all of the arts concerned, entailed taking stock of the state of pedagogy by field. As far

as I was concerned, it was first necessary to revisit the prospects in the relationship, already quite timeworn, between cinema and pedagogy.[9] The latter has long approached cinema primarily as a language and an ideological vehicle. I myself have contributed extensively to a linguistic model of pedagogy, but always with an extreme distrust with regard to those approaches that are oriented toward, above all else, the famous "ideological riposte," in the name of developing the critical mind, to the detriment of cinematic specificity. For several years, through my words and by producing a somewhat different set of tools,[10] I campaigned for the idea that it was time to reverse the outlook and to consider cinema primarily as an art. A symposium in Toulouse, in 1992, had already given me occasion to clarify this idea: "Perhaps we should begin – though it won't be an easy task, pedagogically – by thinking of film not as an object, but as the final imprint of a creative process, and by thinking of cinema as an art. To think of film as the trace of an act of creation, not as an object to be read and decoded, but rather one in which each shot is like a painter's brushstroke, allowing us to begin to comprehend his process of creation. These two perspectives are rather different."[11] I was convinced that, in the years to come, the priority

9 A valuable doctoral dissertation by Francis Desbarats, titled *Origines, conditions et perspectives idéologiques de l'enseignement du cinéma dans les lycées* (The ideological origins, conditions, and outlook of cinema education in secondary schools), Université de Toulouse Le Mirail, Ecole Supérieure d'audiovisuel, defended in December 2001, masterfully recounts this history.
10 *Le cinéma en jeu* (Cinema at play), a book and cassette

tape published in 1992 by L'Institut de l'image d'Aix-en-Provence; *Le cinéma, une histoire de plans* (Cinema, a story in shots), volume 1, 47 minutes, 1998 and volume 2, 61 minutes, 1999, two cassette tapes released by Agat Films and Les enfants du cinéma.
11 Alain Bergala, "Quelque chose de flambant neuf" (Something brand new), *Les Colloques de Cinémémoire 1991 et 1992*, Editions de la Cinémathèque de Toulouse.

should be placed on the approach that would treat cinema as an art (the creation of the new), over the canonical approach that regarded cinema as a vehicle for meaning and ideology (the retreading of what has already been said and known) – even if, for all that, it wasn't necessary to renounce a linguistic approach to cinema, in an absurd mechanical reversal.

The second thread of this "cinema hypothesis" is concerned with the relationship between the critical approach, the "reading" of films, and the enactment, the realization of the creative act. I am increasingly convinced that there is not, on the one hand, a pedagogy of the spectator that would necessarily, by its nature, be limited to reading, to deciphering, to the formation of the critical mind, and, on the other hand, a pedagogy of the filmmaker, of praxis. There could instead be a pedagogy centered on the act of creation that occurs both when one watches films and when one directs films. Obviously, it is this generalized pedagogy of creation that we would be called upon to implement in a mode of education treating cinema as an art. Looking at a painting while asking oneself the questions that the painter would have asked, trying to share in his doubts and his creative feeling, is not the same thing as looking at a painting while restricting oneself to the feelings of a spectator.

Vladimir Nabokov, who was at once a very great writer, an astute literary analyst, and a great teacher (a fact to which his published lectures attest), once explained to his students his goal in teaching literature: "I have tried to make you into good readers, who read not with the childish objective of identifying with the characters of the book, nor with the adolescent objective of learning how to live, nor with the academic objective of giving yourself over to generalizations. I have tried to teach you to read books for their form, for their vision, for their art. I have tried to teach you to feel a small thrill of artistic satisfaction, to partake not in the feelings of the book's characters, but in the feelings of its author – the joys and the challenges of creation. We have not glossed over books, or talked about books; we have gone to the center of this or that masterpiece, to the very heart of the subject."

Here Nabokov defined, with great urgency, what we should aspire to in approaching cinema as an art: to teach students to become spectators who experience the feeling of creation itself.

III

State of Things, States of Mind

THE PEDAGOGICAL TRADITION OF CINEMA-AS-LANGUAGE

The cinema has long been regarded, in the French pedagogical tradition, as a language first and foremost. Approaching a film as a "work of art" was primarily the task of the Ciné-clubs, when the latter were not giving too much sway to the grave sin of "contentism". There are two principal reasons for this division.

The first is a historical coincidence. The hegemonic moment of the language sciences (linguistics, semiology, semiotics) coincided in France with the rise in power of the idea of cinema in schools. The fear of educators faced with this new subject area, film, for which they had not been trained, caused them to cling to more familiar models of analysis that they were already practicing, notably in the study of literature. I will not linger here on a truism: the undeniable success of the problematic of "cinematic adaptation" falls within the same defensive and reassuring reflex. Beginning with the known in an effort to approach the unknown is the opposite of exposing students to art-as-otherness, and generally leads to an evasion of cinema's real singularity. The fear of otherness often leads to the annexation of a new territory with the old, in the manner of colonialism, seeing in the new domain only what one already knew how to see in the old. Cinema has precisely the opposite vocation: to cause us to share experiences which, without cinema, would remain foreign to us; that is, to give us access to otherness.

This preeminence of cinema's linguistic aspect was often the doing of teachers with good intentions, understandably eager to shield the use of cinema in the classroom against the constant threat of the instrumentalization of films that would entail choosing and watching them according to the only possible application of their subject, in the study of history or literature for example. Against the reigning contentism, educators frequently mounted a linguistic imperialism in which one was no longer allowed to use films as a starting point to talk about the world. I remain convinced that "language-ism" is a lesser evil in comparison to the instrumentalization of films, insofar as it leads more easily to a consideration of the specificity and the artistic quality of the film object. But language-ism can easily come down to a denial of the reality of cinema as an impure art – that is, as "language written from reality," in Pasolini's words. We also miss out on an essential part of cinema if we don't talk about the world that film puts before our eyes at the same time that we're analyzing the way in which it reconstructs that world and shows it to us. Pasolini said that cinema is simply "the 'written' manifestation of a natural, total language, which is the acting of reality."[12] Language-ism amputates one of the essential dimensions of cinema, one which distinguishes it from the other arts: the act of "representing reality by way of reality."

The second reason that has driven educators to privilege the cinema-as-language approach is rooted in a solid French tradition of secular education: the priority given, in the driving mission of primary schools, to the development of children's critical minds, and to "ideological debate." The pedagogical illusion has long consisted of a belief that interpretation was the best way to develop the critical mind in children, beginning with small-scale networks of analysis. According to this belief, it would be sufficient to conduct, three times a year, in class, a persuasive analysis of a film or a scene, which students visibly accepted, for teachers to convince themselves that their students "would never watch TV in the same way again." This view requires a rather angelic idea of the power ratio between pedagogical intervention and the firepower of the media and our sonic and visual environment.

This two-pronged approach – linguistic (with regard to the production of meaning) and ideologically defensive – is rarely compatible with an approach that is sensitive to cinema as a plastic and sonic art (and I really mean fully sonic, not just referring to dialogue, as a vehicle of meaning) where textures, materials,

lights, rhythms, and harmonies all count at least as much as linguistic parameters.

THE TRACKING SHOT IS A MORAL ISSUE

I myself was an heir and disciple, during my twelve years of activity as a critic, of the henceforth historic principle put forward by *Cahiers du cinéma* asserting that "the tracking shot is a matter of morality." This theory found its most radical formulation in Jacques Rivette's text on *Kapo*,[13] a film by Gillo Pontecorvo, where the young critic bases his moral judgment on an analysis of one shot in the film, which he deems emblematic of the film's ignominy, in which a prisoner in a concentration camp has just committed suicide: "Observe, however, the shot in *Kapo* where Riva kills herself by throwing herself on the electrified barbed-wire fence: the man who decides, at that moment, to make a tracking shot ahead in order to reframe the dead body from a low angle, taking care to precisely inscribe the raised hand in the angle of its final composition – this man is deserving of only the most profound contempt."

Rivette's decision to base his judgment on a shot from the film belongs to a critical strategy whose pedagogical efficacy is undeniable. The invocation of a localized body of proof wins over the reader's conviction more easily than a general judgment on the film. But it would be a mistake to believe that, merely by analyzing

12 Pier Paolo Pasolini, *Heretical Empiricism*, trans. Ben Lawton and Louise K. Barnett, Bloomington: Indiana University Press, 1988, p. 205.
13 Jacques Rivette, "De l'abjection," *Cahiers du cinéma* n. 120, June 1961.

the famous tracking shot from *Kapo*, Rivette concluded that the entire film was contemptible. Things never transpire that way for the spectator: I imagine that he first experienced global feelings of disillusionment and the shame of being the spectator of a film that aestheticizes horror. The incriminating shot simply came at just the right moment to crystalize an opinion that had already been established over the course of the film. And Rivette was in a position to experience this feeling of repulsion by virtue of having already seen a very great number of films, and having long pondered the question of a formal morality in cinema – which must have been a perennial and daily topic of discussion at *Cahiers du cinéma*. André Bazin had already formulated it in another foundational text: "Montage Interdit" [Montage Prohibited]. Serge Daney, coming back to Rivette's text in a definitive piece published just after his death,[14] "The Tracking Shot in *Kapo*," wrote: "I would definitely have nothing to do, nothing to share with anybody who wasn't immediately upset by the abjection of 'the tracking shot in *Kapo*.'" Daney, who abused neither hyperbole nor the "lived experience" argument, emphasized the verb "upset" so as to make his point perfectly clear: the abjection of *Kapo* is something that is upsetting above all, and Rivette is the one who found the words to convey this sentiment.

On the same occasion, Daney wrote that, contrary to the adage that allows "to each his own," there might in fact be something inexorable, between individuals and in the social sphere, residing in this question of taste. Taste plays an essential discriminatory role in social life as well as in one's own emotional life. When I speak of "taste" here, I am not referring to those small differences on which we can amiably converse in a homogeneous setting – minor disagreements within a general consensus about essential values that is the basis for, say, the petit-bourgeois tastes that define the films that it is necessary to have seen in order to belong to a given social class. I am talking about the differences in taste that are truly divisive in the social realm, differences that downgrade an individual's social standing more reliably than gaps in knowledge, so that a person who announces a sincere and innocent taste for a terrible reproduction of a painting, for example, instantly excludes himself from a social and cultural universe to which he does not belong.

As for the affective realm, in friendship or in love, a disagreement of taste can be more radically divisive than a divergence of opinion. In another piece,[15] Daney describes a soirée that he hosted where he was preparing to watch, along with a young man with whom he was probably in love, Rossellini's *The Flowers of St. Francis*, which happened to be airing that evening on a television channel. He wondered with anguish what would happen, no doubt with regard to his own feelings towards the young man, if the latter were to reveal himself to be absolutely resistant to the film: could he,

14 Serge Daney, "The Tracking Shot in *Kapo*." trans. Laurent Kretzschmar, *Senses of Cinema* n. 30, February 2004.
15 *Roberto Rossellini*, special issue of *Cahiers du cinéma*, ed. Cahiers du cinéma/Cinémathèque française, 1989.

Daney, become attached to someone who was totally unmoved by Rossellini? The story has a happy ending, for the other man turned out to be immediately affected by the innocent world of the friars filmed by Rossellini. Contrary to the popular dictum, whereas opinions might be debated, tastes cannot be, as they fall too squarely within the jurisdiction of the uniqueness of the individual, of his intimate self, to be negotiable. Any deep divergence in taste injures the self-regard of the person whose taste is rejected.

The pedagogical illusion consists in believing that things could happen this way, in three phases that unfold obediently in chronological order. Phase One: you analyze a shot or a sequence, as Rivette did with *Kapo*. Phase Two: you judge the film on the basis of this analysis. Phase Three: you thus gradually accumulate an appraisal based on analysis. It is obvious that things never happen in this way: it is taste, formed by having seen numerous films and the designations that accompany them, that gives rise "little by little" to whatever judgment might occasionally be cast on such-and-such a film. And it's this judgment, insofar as you have felt it globally in the course of screening a film, which enables you to see and analyze the greatness, the mediocrity, or the abjection of a shot or a sequence. The tracking shot is indeed a matter of morals, but in order to discern the morality of a tracking shot, one must have already seen many tracking shots of all kinds, and must have amassed in advance what is simply called an appreciation of cinema.

Pedagogy, as we know, devises procedures that allow individuals to "save time" on the "natural" unfolding of the learning process. All education is, of course, a simulation. But this simulation must respect both its subject – film – without reducing that subject to its mere contours, and the means by which it can wind its way into the consciousness of a person, especially when the person in question is a child. It is thus possible to slightly "accelerate" the process of building one's understanding of a formal ethics, but never to "force" it in a dogmatic – and symbolically ineffective and even dangerous – way.

Serge Daney slightly accelerates his own thought process when he makes a comparison between the shot from *Kapo* and another shot, sampled from Mizoguchi's *Ugetsu*. In this shot, where another young woman meets her death during wartime, in the middle of nowhere, Mizoguchi's camera is nearly oblivious at the moment of his heroine's death, and very nearly misses it, showing us "the event in the process of transpiring as an event, that is, unavoidably and obliquely." The juxtaposition of these two shots in Serge Daney's mind took time, and was not pointed out to him by anyone. He had doubtlessly been ruminating for several months on Rivette's text when, unexpectedly, in Studio Bertrand, he stumbled upon the shot of Miyagi's death and was, he tells us, literally "pierced, torn" by it. Such juxtapositions might very well take years, or might never even materialize. It's here that the *passeur*, to borrow an expression from Serge Daney,[16] plays the role of accelerating thought, of teaching, by helping us to save time by setting up the demonstrative comparison between these two shots.

The illusion would be to believe, on the basis of this convincing example, that one might be able not to accelerate but to totally reverse the normal process of acquiring opinions and tastes with regard to cinema. The illusion would be to believe, ultimately, out of pedagogical naiveté, and in order to reassure oneself, that a formal analysis establishing a striking shortcut between form and judgment (as we saw with the tracking shot in *Kapo*) could forever arm students and allow them to distinguish between a good and a bad film. No one will ever save enough time to form a personal taste upon which the criteria of judgment might be propped up with any kind of durability.

CINEMA AS ART

The idea of response-based pedagogy, aimed primarily at developing critical thinking skills, belongs to a conception of cinema as a *bad object*. If there's any hope of bringing cinema into

16 I want to note in passing—speaking of Daney, who "invented" the term in this usage, referring to an agent of transmission—that this lovely word *passeur* is today used quite loosely, to fit any occasion. A *passeur* is someone who gives of himself, who accompanies his passengers in the boat or up the mountain, who takes the same risks as those temporarily in his charge. Today everyone uses *passeur* to whitewash or cheaply ennoble labors or concerns in which there is neither risk nor any kind of passage. André Bazin, Henri Agel, Jean Douchet, Serge Daney, Philippe Arnaud, and Alain Philippon were *passeurs*, to name just a few.

schools, it's on the condition that cinema is treated as an object worthy of study – that is, as an art above all. I have never understood the fact that one can, in good faith, encourage the study of "bad" films in the classroom, under the pretext of developing the perennially celebrated critical thinking skills. Would it ever occur to anyone to knowingly introduce a "bad" painting in class, a crude imitation or cheap reproduction, in order to learn, from its analysis, what makes a good painting? Life (in and out of the classroom) is too short to justify wasting time and energy on watching and analyzing bad films – especially insofar as a bad film, even when analyzed as such, necessarily leaves a trace, pollutes one's taste, as soon as it becomes the subject of repeat viewings, instant replays, paused frames: unconscious memory, which makes a mockery of value judgments, retains the bad as well as the good. The reason for this kind of aberration is profound: a teacher wants to recognize that cinema is an art, but from the perspective of his (good) secular conscience, cinema remains first and foremost an ideological vehicle, which ought to be mistrusted from the start.

If a person believes that it is necessary, above all, to learn how to defend oneself against films, that person must first deem cinema dangerous. But the danger identified is always the same essentially ideological threat: films can sneakily, along with a surplus of pleasure, carry harmful values (vindicating violence, racism, sexism, etc.). I have rarely heard allusions to another danger, which might in fact cause damage that is more profound and lasting: the danger of artistic mediocrity or inanity. There is something worse than a bad film: a mediocre film. Schools willingly worry themselves over "bad films," which can have a negative effect on children, while never fearing the ravages of mediocrity. Yet mediocrity is the more widespread and insidious danger by far.

Today, schools can do better by talking about film, first of all, as works of art and culture. Giving students other points of reference and approaching films confidently, without displaying prejudicial distrust, is certainly, nowadays, the best response to bad films. If one is successful, with films whose artistic value is incontestable (if such a thing exists!), in reconstructing something that resembles taste, one will have accomplished more toward fighting bad or dangerous films than by trying, first, to hastily supply some partial tools of defensive criticism. More than ever before, it is a pedagogical illusion to believe that a few short analyses would be enough, independently of any sufficiently consolidated culture, to produce the realization that a film is harmful or bad. Not to mention the naive but intractable belief that a child who takes pleasure in a bad film will, deep down, renounce this personal pleasure as soon as someone has demonstrated to him, even by means of an accurate and well-drawn analysis, that the film is bad or pernicious. It is because he found *Kapo* insufferable, on the basis of a well-established cinematic taste, that Rivette saw and analyzed the shamefulness of the famous shot for the *Cahiers* readers of the time. The formation of this taste,

which alone allowed Rivette to maintain a critical distance with regard to bad films, is problem number one today. Encountering and perpetually engaging with other films is, today, the best retaliation against the firepower of popcorn cinema.

There is a great danger of being misunderstood when one speaks of cinema as an art. It is best to clarify one's meaning so as to avoid any misunderstanding. Obviously I am not referring to all of these films that aspire to "artiness" by flaunting "production values," with luxurious decor and extravagant lighting and camerawork. Artistry in cinema is neither ornamentation nor ostentation, neither conspicuous academicism nor cultural intimidation. The "hartistic," with an aspirated H, is the primary enemy of cinema as a real and specific art form. Great art, in cinema, is the opposite of cinema that exhibits a surplus of artiness. It's the dryness of Rossellini or Bresson. It's the relentless and unpadded rigor of a Hitchcock or a Lang. It's the lucidity of Howard Hawks, the naked tidiness of Kiarostami's films. It's the life that overflows from every shot by Renoir or Fellini. It's each time that emotion and thought are born out of a form, a rhythm, that could not have existed but for cinema.

Primary schools remain massively narrow-minded: they voluntarily screen films, even those whose artistic merit is minimal or nonexistent, merely for the fact that they approach, with a certain generosity of spirit, some big subject which can then be debated among the students. The old notion of the "Screen Files" film screening, where the film is purely a pretext for debating a big subject, is resilient in the national education ministry. The problem is that good films are rarely narrow-minded, which is to say immediately digestible and recyclable in simple and ideologically correct ideas.

A filmmaker worthy of the title is not a filmmaker who makes his film principally in order to say what he has to say on a given subject, even if the subject is one of the utmost importance. The real filmmaker is "engaged by" a question, which his film in turn engages. He is not someone for whom the purpose of filming is to translate into images ideas of which he is already certain, but rather someone who is searching and thinking through the very act of making the film. Filmmakers who already have the answer – and for whom film's task is not to produce, but merely to transmit a preconceived message – instrumentalize cinema. Art that is content to send messages is not art, but a vehicle unworthy of art: the same is true for cinema. *Shoah* is not a great film because it deals with the Holocaust; it is a great film because Claude Lanzmann pursued, in every sense of the term, the question of the representation of the Shoah in cinema, and attacked from behind all of the accepted ideas on the question, inventing a cinema that would permit him to think differently on the subject, and demonstrating with his film the perpetual inventiveness of the form itself.

In 1960, when Godard set out to film *Le Petit Soldat*, the least you could say was that he lacked clear ideas about the Algerian Question even at this decisive turning point in the war, and more than once he verged dangerously on abysses where he might have lost his way. Rarely, since the Rossellini of *Rome, Open City* and *Germany, Year Zero*, has such a hot-off-the-presses film been made by a young man who did not know what he had to say, who did not hide his fascination with the worst theories of the time, but who had simply perceived that this taboo subject was the crucial subject of the moment, and that making a film would perhaps allow him to escape from his own confusion and his bad temptations. *Le Petit Soldat*, whichever way you look at it, remains today an ideologically dangerous film, whose message is no clearer than it was forty years ago, but in which we see a filmmaker at work who has an absolute respect for and belief in cinema and its powers of elucidation and thought. It is a film that has remained full of life, contradictory, irritating and fascinating, full of ingenuity, that continues to be thought-provoking more than forty years after its production, while so many narrow-minded films, made with the iron fist of ideological or political convictions, are now regarded as nothing more than cumbersome chores, unworthy of cinema and of thought, long since braindead. In cinema, the verdict of time comes at a very accelerated pace, in relation to other arts, separating works that continue to remain vital from those that lose their vitality once they cease to benefit from the meagre effect of contemporaneity, which leads us to have difficulty distinguishing between the life of a film and the life that surrounds us, of which the film is a reflection.

Narrow-minded films, strong in their convictions, even justly so, are strewn across the graveyard of films whose lives and resonances have vanished. According to Hou Hsiao-hsien, the best antidote consists in always privileging what one sees, at the moment of shooting the film, over what one thinks or the idea one has about it, and the phrasing of his films confirms that he is right: "… one must be careful not to end up plastering one's ideas onto the things that one is filming, as so many directors do. The result: there is no longer any room to breathe, nothing more happens. Even if, like everyone else, I have my own opinions, I do not seek to flaunt them, but rather to show the light of their presence. Then, each viewer, seeing this presence and the light that it radiates, can interpret it according to his own understanding."[17] Jean-Marie Straub, as much a political filmmaker as exists today, once told me during an interview that for a shot to be worth the effort, there must be "something that burns in the shot." What burns is the life and presence of the things and people that inhabit it. And what if, in schools, people talked more about this life that burns or doesn't burn in cinematic shots, rather than always talking about this "grammar" of images that has never existed, and about the "big subjects" that suffocate cinema?

In October 1959, in the 100th issue of *Cahiers du cinéma*, whose cover had been designed by Jean Cocteau ("le 100 [cent] d'un poète," a play on the title of Cocteau's film *Le Sang d'un poète*), Claude Chabrol had already put mis-chievous pen to paper to defend small-scale subject matter against the "idiots" – his word – who were already rallying large numbers in support of big subjects: "In my opinion," he concluded, "there are no big or small subjects, because the smaller a subject becomes, the more one treats it with grandeur. In truth, there is nothing but the truth." Robert Bresson, for his part, correctly believed that a big subject distances a filmmaker from his humble human experience: "A small subject can provide the pretext for many profound combinations. Avoid subjects that are too vast or too remote, in which nothing warns you when you are going astray. Or else take from them only what can be mingled with your life and belongs to your experience."[18] Indeed, the pattern repeats itself too often to attribute it to simple coincidence: we see good filmmakers succumb to academicism and grandiloquence for having criticized the "big subjects" where they lost their sense of moderation and their identities as men and artists, if not their souls. Educators continue to love big subjects for reasons that are at times good in terms of general and civic education (initiating conversations about… war, racism, etc.), but these conversations do not necessarily do credit to cinema, nor, in certain cases, do they even simply respect it as an art.

17 *Hou Hsiao-hsien*, edited by Jean-Michel Frodon, collected essays, ed. Cahiers du cinéma, 1999.
18 Robert Bresson, *Notes on Cinematography*, trans. Jonathan Griffin, New York: Urizen Books, 1977, p. 22.

CINEMA AND THE AUDIOVISUAL:
THE TROUBLE WITH "AND"

When Serge Daney, ever himself, was invited to participate in a run-of-the-mill symposium in the "theater and cinema," "music and cinema," "cinema and history," "painting and cinema" genre, he maintained that he could never be satisfied with a conference framed around "and." In film education, the two "ands" that come up most frequently are those that associate cinema with literature and with audiovisual media. The "and" in "cinema and television" has for decades done more bad than good in the French education system. It is based on a generous and wholly defensive idea: the educator charged with teaching cinema would be tasked with the primary objective of developing critical thinking skills, and the most necessary of necessities would be to develop these critical thinking skills with regard to television. There is nothing wrong with this premise, except that such a critical approach to television would logically fall more within the realm of civic instruction than of arts education.

When I took charge of the cinema portion of this project for promoting the arts in primary schools, the rigid phrase "cinema-and-audiovisual media" was terribly in effect at the ministry, like everywhere else in the field of pedagogy. My position simply consisted in affirming that it is necessary, on the one hand, to renounce this overly vague word "audiovisual," as it's impossible to know, for example, whether it encompasses slideshow montages with accompanying soundtracks or the programming on French television channel TF1,

which evidently have nothing in common, or all the resurgent techniques of combining images and sounds. And on the other hand, if art was the objective of the project, I saw little of it on television, apart from whatever might fall precisely under the domain of a cinematic imagination. I thus tried (though bad habits of vocabulary die hard, and rally like weeds against any attempt at change) to eliminate the word "audiovisual" from anything having to do specifically with cinema, and made an appeal for a radical separation between an approach that would treat cinema as an art (including whatever cinematic material might be found on television) and a critical approach to television in its specificity. For the Mission, an "audio-visual" adviser thus took responsibility for television as a specific domain, which, it must be said, was a great relief to me.

It was indeed with the word "and" that things became muddled. Unfortunately, cinema's status being what it is in the education system, it is hard even now to see who, other than a teacher with a competency in cinema, could be tasked with taking this approach to television. But just because there is a tradition of teaching history and geography together does not mean that there is the least confusion between the two fields. The same cannot be said of cinema and television. The idea that muddles everything and prevents any serious consideration of the question is the false evidence suggesting that a given methodology for teaching cinema would provide tools to arm students against television. The capital-i Image does not exist, except as a pedagogical fantasy of an all-powerful retort: it would suffice to know how to analyze the Image in order to be capable of analyzing all images. Alas, the absolute weapon is a fantasy, and one must look further to find methodologies that are sufficiently specific to have any efficiency. Even in terms of the debate, the gardener knows perfectly well that every pest requires its own specific pesticide.

Let's suppose, as a starting point, that television is nothing but a piece of hardware and a medium of distribution. It is strictly impossible to place everything that it distributes under the same label. Its content must be divided into two large categories: there's the content that falls under the umbrella of the cinematic imagination (films, made-for-TV movies, documentaries, ads, clips), which adopts the codes, the production and post-production methods of cinema; and there's content that belongs, in a word, to the televisual apparatus (variety programs, mind-numbing games of all sorts, talk shows, news shows, live sports, political interviews). If there is a specifically televisual imagination, it belongs exclusively to the second category. These two kinds of production distributed by television have in common merely the hardware and the shared site of reception, while they appeal to two radically different imaginative modes and spectatorial postures.

The tools that allow us to engage with the first category (cinematic content) are of no use in analyzing the second (televisual content). The most intelligent analysis of framing and lighting by Orson Welles or Jean Vigo will never provide an instrument suitable for ana-

lyzing one of those nauseating shows (psychobabble talk shows or reality programs) in which any television viewer could be, unfortunately for him, hero for a day. I do not see any interest or pedagogical benefit whatsoever in mixing the methodologies for engaging with these two kinds of objects, as their combination would yield a rather unappetizing result, not unlike mixing water and oil.

The other major danger of the "and" between cinema and television is that it distorts from the outset the relationship in question. Television, even and especially for those who fiercely defend the necessity of teaching it in primary schools, is largely experienced as a bad object, insidious, dangerous, harmful, against which people must learn to defend themselves. The narrow-minded pedagogical ideal is thus to mould, through appropriate critical training, what used to be called an "active viewer." I have never really believed in this notion, for two reasons. The first reason is the criterion of pleasure: the most well-supported of discourses can never gain ground against a child's feeling that a particular show has brought him pleasure, when an adult is attempting to demonstrate how questionable it is. The second reason is the balance of power: it requires either a great deal of naiveté or an excess of pedagogical ardor to seriously believe that a few meagre hours spent analyzing the televisual apparatus – which returns in force every evening on the television itself, with all its powers of seduction and consensus – would suffice to arm the young television viewer for life with impervious critical thinking skills, which, according to the formula established by self-congratulatory pedagogues, will ensure that "he will never watch television in the same way again," that is, in the way that he watched before the miraculous pedagogical intervention. Alas, things are not so simple, and, in terms of the debate, I hardly see anything but the patient and permanent formation of one's taste, rooted in beautiful things, which might have opportunities, even minimally, to act as antidotes to the crass nonsense and aggressive ugliness of the majority of television shows that do not belong to the cinematic imagination. There is beauty in clips and advertisements, but it owes everything to cinema.

Because it, too, is "dangerous," cinema – which I want to emphasize is a wholly more "genuine" bad object – would fall under the same kind of analysis and the same teaching methodologies as television. The "and" in "cinema and television" has the major negative effect of lumping together what is unambiguously a bad object with a category that must be regarded as a good object in order to bear any meaning. The only symbolic benefit to be had by bringing cinema into the classroom is that it carries a familiar assertion to its logical conclusion: in art, the priority is to learn to love, and we know from the lovely title of Jean Douchet's collected writings that criticism, too, can be seen as "the art of loving."[19]

19 Jean Douchet, *L'Art d'aimer*, collected writings, ed. Cahiers du cinéma, August 1987.

At this point in the debate, there is always someone who takes the floor, with the self-assurance of one who is on the right track, to bring down from the attic the counterexample, worn down after decades of good and loyal service, of research by Jean-Christophe Averty, who was without a doubt the only person to try to imagine a creative mode that would take into account the specificity of the television screen. Video art, as everyone knows, likewise interrogates the medium of the cathode-ray tube, but it does not really have a place, to say the least, on television, though the latter would be its most natural distribution format. In the end, it's sports programming that has given shape to the pleasures and the specifically interesting, and often beautiful, forms of television. Doubtlessly, this was the context that gave rise to new emotions, unprecedented in cinema, integrating an open, non-cinematic storyline (the rules themselves of tennis or football) and an aesthetic belonging to the apparatus of live television. What remains of the "specifically televisual" has today, in large part, become pure nightmare: hysterical set pieces, talk shows where "human" dialogue no longer has a place, poor brainwashed John Does, humiliated and happy about it, placed by their own consent in a setting saturated with the densest stupidity, lobotomized good humor, and obligatory moments of emotion.

Must we really make room, in schools, for all this misery? We would do more for children by showing them a shot by Kiarostami than by spending two hours dissecting who-knows-what televisual slop.

35

IV

Cinema in Childhood

ASTONISHMENT AND MYSTERY

Serge Daney wrote in 1988: "While speaking for several hours to willing listeners, I realize that I am circling the 'hard core' of films that, as Jean Louis Schefer said, 'have seen my childhood,' or rather my adolescence as an innocent cinephile."[20]

These lines aptly express the determining factor at play in the moment, during childhood or adolescence, when a person encounters the films that are essential in the formation of his relationship to cinema. A person will carry these films, limited in number, with him all his life, each in his own way, like a sort of long-lasting travel stipend. All cinephiles remember films that affixed the love of cinema to their bodies.

These films do not necessarily bear a direct relationship with the cinema that they are going to love later on. In the generation that Serge Daney was referring to, you could become a great Bressonian, like Philippe Arnaud, after having been disturbed by cinema, at the age of nine, upon seeing *War of the Buttons*.[21] The elements at play there, like a "big bang," do not fall under any distinction of taste or culture, but rather are aspects of the encounter, in its uniqueness, its unpredictability, and its power to astonish. It resides in the instanta-

neous certainty, of which Schefer[22] and Daney spoke, that this film, which was waiting for me, knows something about my mysterious relationship to the world, something about which I myself am ignorant but which the film contains like a secret to decipher.

Nothing afterwards will take the place of this first emotion that marks every true encounter with the cinema. There exists for each of us, always following Daney's formulation, a handful of formative films (for Daney, the films that he viewed between 1959 and 1964, thus between the ages of 15 and 20), "and films that came later," he writes, "about which I say, today, that I would have (or might have) loved them when I was younger. It's a list of many 'astonishments.' Just once, a note is hit, and it is unforgettable."

Our cinematic imagination is not formed in a homogenous or continuous way throughout our lives. There is a "starter set" of films that will largely delineate the contours of our areas of attraction and interest. Daney pursues his

20 Serge Daney, *L'exercice a été profitable, Monsieur*, P.O.L., 1993.
21 Philippe Arnaud, *Les paupières du visible*, Yellow Now, coll. Côté cinéma, 2001.
22 Jean Louis Schefer, *L'homme ordinaire du cinéma*, Petite bibliothèque des Cahiers, 1997.

hypothesis to the point of speculating that there are films seen "too late," unable to achieve the determining impact they could have had on us if we had encountered them during this decisively formative period of a few years: "Whatever is not seen 'in time' will never truly be seen."[23]

When the first list (containing the first impressions that "hit the unforgettable note") is closed for good, no film can ever be added to it retroactively, even among those films that would have certainly had a place on it and that will forever remain in limbo, excluded from the hard core of films that made us devotees of cinema. These films, encountered "too late," will remain partially undisclosed, like a photo that was never fully developed, which will forever be too pale, without the contrast and the depth that it would have taken on.

From this assessment it follows that it is vitally important to encounter good films – those which will leave a mark that lasts a lifetime – at the right moment. In 1993, the book *Cet enfant de cinéma* collected a hundred people's first memories of cinema, with contributions from anonymous moviegoers as well as film professionals and other writers. The book offered confirmation that the important encounters, when it comes to cinema, are often with films that are one step ahead of the awareness that we have of ourselves and our relationship to life. At the time of the encounter, we're content to register the enigma with surprise, and to hold it responsible for the force of

the shock and distress we feel. The process of elucidation will come later, and might last twenty, thirty years, or a lifetime. The film works on us quietly, its shockwaves spread slowly. Philippe Arnaud wrote in his book: "Every image enlightens, during the symbolic famine of childhood: it not only illuminates its own meaning, but, in the instantaneous anticipation of an entity that is foreign to us, it foreshadows a possibility of ourselves through which we are chosen: it is a process of colonization by necessary images that indicate and compose a kind of destiny that awaits us, a knowledge that is disconcerting because it precedes us. The images are always imprinted inexorably, such that we know that their contents concern us without understanding why."

We can require learning, but we cannot require being moved. We all know that with the books, films, musical pieces that have mattered in our lives, we have encountered them individually, on an intimate scale, each in his own way, even if the encounter took place in what appeared to be a collective context or an institutional setting. When primary schools make learning a requirement – with the aim of qualifying students for their future integration in the social order, which will one day be required of them – their primary objective is certainly not to foster the possibility of a decisive individual encounter with a work. This encounter represents more an initiation than a learning process, and schools can never dictate nor guarantee that it will occur. Like any true encounter, it might also never happen at all in the force of its personal revelation and shock.

23 Serge Daney, *Trafic* n. 4, Autumn 1992, P.O.L.

Schools, however, do have a non-negligible role to play in this business. And this role has four parts.

FIRST: SETTING UP THE POSSIBILITY FOR AN ENCOUNTER WITH FILMS

How might one facilitate the child's exposure to such an encounter? In the realm of cinema, today, that means concretely deploying every apparatus and every possible strategy to place children – the greatest number of children and teenagers – in the presence of films that they will have less and less of a chance of encountering anywhere other than in school (or in a movie theater connected to a school). Orchestrating the encounter is a grave responsibility. We all know that the right conditions, in terms of desire, have often appeared to be precisely the wrong conditions: films seen covertly, often, in a context where we were not intended to see them, or even guiltily, or while playing truant from school or work, like Antoine Doinel in *The 400 Blows*.

This responsibility is even larger if we believe, like Gracq, that everything is in play from the very first encounter, and that the consequences are irrevocable, for better and for worse: "... I think that ..., from the first eye contact that two people exchange, a certain vocal inflection that imposes itself, as insidious and as fatal as poetic inspiration, attaches to them forever, for better or for worse – or for complete indifference."[24] The worst, when it comes to encountering a work of art, is the indifference that Gracq mentions; all the rest – violent rejection, difficulty in engaging, irritation

– is still an access road that has been opened. We all have memories of works that we resisted for a long time, sometimes violently, and which we ended up adding, unexpectedly, to the group of films that matter in a lifetime.

SECOND: APPOINTING, INITIATING, AND BECOMING THE PASSEUR

We have all had the experience, in a time when the cultural thread between generations was less ragged, of meeting in our scholarly pursuits a "charismatic" teacher whose contagious enthusiasm enabled us to encounter such-and-such a book or author and appropriate their enthusiasm. This chance of passing down one's own passions and convictions is not necessarily part of the profession, nor of the talent required to be a good teacher. There are those who even see it as a liability, to risk weakening the free will and critical thinking of the student by placing him under an emotional influence that would likely incur all sorts of intimidations and biases. This process of initiation under the personalized direction of a "master" is merely an adjacent path alongside the major highway of education that does not demand so much of an educator. But what kind of real impact can we expect from an approach to art that is not, at the same time, an initiation?

When an adult voluntarily takes the risk, whether by conviction or by personal love of an art, to become a "messenger," his own symbolic status changes, he abandons for a moment his role as an educator, as that role has

24 *Cet enfant du cinéma que nous avons été*, op. cit.

been defined and delimited by the institution, in order to take up a way of speaking with and interacting with his students that is rooted in a different part of himself, more vulnerable, where his personal tastes come into play, as well as his more intimate relationship to one work of art or another, where the "I" that can be so harmful in the role of the teacher becomes practically indispensable to a good initiation. It's all in the difference between what the institution has a right to expect from an educator teaching a class in his discipline, and what that educator can create as an "other" space and as a different kind of relationship with his students when he frames it as "his" education, in the arts or elsewhere, in order to act as *passeur*, initiator, in an artistic field that he has chosen voluntarily because it moves him personally. This difference, even poorly maintained, with a clear awareness of both roles, this slippage can benefit everyone, teacher and students alike. It's the difference between training in the arts and an arts education, between teaching and initiation – or, as Godard would say, between the rule and the exception.

THIRD: LEARNING TO GO TO THE MOVIES
After the big bang of the encounter, if it happens, the role of the school should be to facilitate flexible, continuous, lively, individualized access to the film, and to introduce children to a mode of reading that is creative, and not merely analytical or critical. This approach will be incomplete, consisting of back-and-forths, of diligently attending to selections that the child has seized on, of revisiting, of conversa-

tions with other "admirers" of this work, sometimes of iconoclasm.

The school must accept that the process takes time, sometimes years, and that the school's role is not to compete with the laws and functions of entertainment. On the contrary, its role is to accept the otherness of the artistic encounter, and to allow the necessary strangeness of the work of art to make its slow progress on its own, through a long process of impregnation for which the school must simply create the best conditions possible.

The idea of the creative spectator is a strong idea, unfamiliar in schools, where there is a tendency to pass a bit too quickly into analysis, without giving the artwork time to resonate and to reveal itself to each student according to his sensibility.

Nabokov wrote: "Curiously enough, one cannot *read* a book: one can only reread it. A good reader, a major reader, an active and creative reader is a rereader. And I shall tell you why. When we read a book for the first time the very process of laboriously moving our eyes from left to right, line after line, page after page, this complicated physical work upon the book, the very process of learning in terms of space and time what the book is about, this stands between us and artistic appreciation. When we look at a painting we do not have to move our eyes in a special way even if, as in a book, the picture contains elements of depth and development. The element of time does not really enter in a first contact with a painting. In reading a book, we must have time to acquaint ourselves with it. We have no physical organ (as we have the eye in regard to a painting) that takes in the whole picture and then can enjoy its details. But at a second, or third, or fourth reading we do, in a sense, behave towards a book as we do towards a painting."[25]

As with books, so it goes with cinema: our first viewing of a film requires following from one shot to the next, from one scene to the next, during the limited span of an hour and a half. The viewing is largely driven by the necessity of understanding the story, not confusing the characters, situating each new scene in space and time relative to the scene that precedes it. Indeed, this first viewing is necessarily dedicated, for the most part, to "reading" the story, to making sense of it. It is only upon revisiting the film later that one can experience, in a more leisurely way, without the tense fear of not understanding what's going on, the elements of true artistic beauty. I have always personally been anxious, going into a film with a complicated screenplay and a large cast of characters, that I will not be able to understand the story, that I will fail to keep track of the identities and roles of the characters – none of which seem to pose a problem for the "normal," non-cinephile spectators around me, perhaps (according to a hypothesis that does not involve a humiliating congenital weakness on my part) because they are utterly, innocently, immersed in a transparent reception of the film, undisturbed by the worries that distract and trouble me.

I am not certain that the first viewing of a film is the one which allows the viewer to be most receptive to every element in the perception of the film, which later, partial viewings will reveal to him. This must remain a priority in any effort to approach cinema as an art. This sensitive approach to cinema could relax the inhibitions of educators: it demands no special ability other than the ability to be attentive to what is concretely visible onscreen and audible on the soundtrack, which the teacher can then discuss on equal footing with the students, initially. Even at university level, this step, which any approach to film should take as a starting point, is sometimes breezed through by "readers" who are too hasty to decode and interpret.

FOURTH: DRAWING CONNECTIONS BETWEEN FILMS

The primary school classroom is the best context – if not the only context – in which to fight against this rampant amnesia to which we are becoming accustomed thanks to new modes of film consumption, and the best context in which to approach films as belonging to a chain of artworks, of which even the most novel and liberated film is but a single link. A major function of primary schools, today more problematic than ever, consists in tracing certain common themes between the artworks of the present and of the past, forging connections, sketching out genealogies, without which any full-on confrontation with the work of art has every chance of being stifled, even

25 Vladimir Nabokov, *Lectures on Literature*, ed. Fredson Bowers, New York: Harcourt Brace Jovanovich, 1980, p. 3.

if the art is of a high quality. Without these connections, a student is liable to experience a series of emotional shocks which, in isolation, will never amount to knowledge, but merely to a patchwork of orphan films. Cultural knowledge is nothing more than this ability to relate the painting or film that one is presently seeing, or the book that one is reading, to other paintings, other films, other books. And in the case of true cultural knowledge, this ability opens up the pleasure of finding one's way in the fraught network of artworks as they appear before us, most often in disarray, and of understanding how every work of art is inhabited by what preceded it, and by its contemporaries, in the art from which it emerged, and in the neighboring arts, even when its author knew nothing of them or rejected them outright.

The criterion of mere emotion or of pleasure "full-stop" (I was moved by a film, and that was enough) is always a means of reducing one's relationship with art to consumption, pure and simple. To experience one's own humanity through an artwork is to relate oneself to the chain of which the work is a part. This should not prevent a person from experiencing pleasure "full-stop," but the pleasure of connection gives us access to something more universal than the fleeting satisfaction of our own little "me, here and now." An awareness of this chain is, today, the most difficult thing to pass down, because the need for it is not spontaneously felt in a "channel-surfing" culture, where you jump from one thing to another

without needing to tie them together, in a series of stimulating and unpredictable distractions, which leave you somewhat dazed, but without much else, other than the memory of the pleasure of exhilaration.

If art's only function is to bring us pleasure, then schools need not concern themselves with it: each person can find the means and the objects that will bring pleasure more quickly and more economically. What's more, all of us – adults and children alike – have at one time or another taken pleasure in some utter inanity on television, knowing perfectly well that such pleasure is pure release. Who among us has not spent a tired evening channel-surfing, when he has had enough of being the cultured, aesthetically correct cinephile? Yet this does not detract from the awareness that there are pleasures of a different nature, whose economy, intensity, and impact are not to be judged on the same terms. There is a pleasure that is unique to children, with which school can have nothing to do. But there is a more established pleasure in one's relationship to a work of art that does not necessarily come about immediately or without effort, and primary school can play an important role in teaching it. An artwork's intelligence – with all due respect to those who whine that "pleasure is killed by analysis" – participates in this artistic pleasure.

ART IS WHAT FIGHTS BACK

Director of photography Dominique Chapuis wrote in *Cet enfant du cinéma*: "I would like it if children could continue to love films that

41

they do not understand at all." I suppose he perceived, even in 1993, that the dictums of nonstop consumption and communication would make it increasingly difficult for children to "consent to" loving films that are the slightest bit resistant. The state of things has not improved in the years since, and has even found passing expression in "youth-speak": "that puts me to sleep" and "that bores me to death" might refer to anything that is not immediately digestible in its entirety, with no effort expended, and "I was glued to my chair" suggests something that captivates instantaneously and induces unflagging compliance.

Simone Weil employs the unusual word "consent." It refers, ultimately, to the act of "consenting to" the work of art, which implies letting go of an initial resistance, or even hostility, within oneself. The attention that the individual ultimately gives to the artwork – that he *consents to* give – was not necessarily given upon initially encountering the work. The artwork that will matter in a person's life is initially resistant, and does not immediately offer itself up with all the attractions of instantaneous seduction belonging to the disposable films that overwhelm screens and media bandwidth every Wednesday.[26] All of these films which one is socially obligated to have seen each week, each month, push back into oblivion its precedents, even if there emerge, from time to time, certain "cult favorites," isolated in memory, where they form an archipelago of sporadic items, solitary blocks in the cultural imagination, but do not necessarily comprise a structured landscape. One of the characteristics

of such socially-requisite "must-see" films is their power of immediate seduction. These films are always-already likable, never putting up any resistance at first glance, upon first viewing, requiring no process of familiarization, utterly digestible.

The selling point of authorial identification that one sees today on posters ("from the director of…" or even "from the producer of…"!) clearly no longer has anything to do with the tradition of auteur theory, where the filmmaker's singularity is placed front-and-center. Every new film by Hitchcock, who was the first director whose name was attached to movies as a selling point, was sure to surprise in relation to the one that came before. Today, it's precisely a matter of guaranteeing to the client that he will find the same product and the same pleasure, in what we might call brand theory.

In *The Gay Science*, Nietzsche writes about this necessary "strangeness" of the true work of art, which is not immediately identifiable, which requires effort and reveals itself to us slowly, which is often a bit off-putting at the moment of the initial encounter, before this strangeness becomes an object of affection.

The equivalent of the "consent" towards a work of art that Simone Weil describes is, in Nietzsche's writing, the "exertion and goodwill" required, upon first encountering an artwork, "to *tolerate* it in spite of its strangeness, to

26 Editor's note: In France, Wednesday is generally the day of the week when new films are released.

be patient with its appearance and expression, and kindhearted about its oddity."[27]

The DVD collection titled "L'Eden Cinéma,"[28] too, consists of "must-see films," but the prescription is of an entirely different order. If the presence of this collection in classrooms or schools means something, it is neither as curriculum nor as canon, but as a means of letting time do its work, teaching students to fully appreciate the artworks in the collection, providing straightforward access to the connections, the genealogies, the multiple interrelationships with other artworks, other cultural fields, that the collection suggests. The ultimate objective of this initiation is not scholarly knowledge, which is within the purview of education, but rather to learn how to love, according to Nietzsche's formulation: "That is how we have *learned to love* all things that we now love. In the end we are always rewarded for our good will, our patience, fairmindedness, and gentleness with what is strange; gradually, it sheds its veil and turns out to be a new and indescribable beauty. That is its *thanks* for our hospitality. Even those who love themselves will have learned it in this way; for there is no other way. Love, too, has to be learned."

27 Friedrich Nietzsche, *The Gay Science*, trans. Walter Kaufmann, New York: Random House, 1974, p. 262.
28 The collection "L'Eden cinéma" was designed to accompany the Five-Year Plan in cinema studies. It was released by Le Seren (formerly CNDP).

TEACHING: CUTTING THE CORD BETWEEN GENERATIONS

I remember the disgust I felt during my childhood and my adolescence every time an adult, even motivated by the best intentions of initiating a conversation, tried to "understand" my tastes down to the most intimately personal detail, to take an interest in something (a book, a film) that I had chosen precisely as "my own," and which I could see clearly did not speak to this well-meaning adult, for I was all too aware that, in the end, he was taking an interest in it merely out of "paternalism" – something which I experienced as a slightly obscene intrusion in my private garden. I promised myself I would never "home in on" the cultural objects selected by my own children, nor by other people's children, unless their selections happened to affect me personally, apart from any cross-generational reason. Today I still feel a very great repugnance any time an adult – whatever his good intentions – homes in on the personal, individual pleasure that a child takes in one film or another. This pleasure does not concern us. Let us give children leave to take pleasure in films that we deem to be rubbish, if only in the name of the horrors that we might have loved before we developed our good taste, little by little, and gradually eliminated the chaff. The pedagogically reactionary person can become dangerous when he runs the risk of offending his students' sensibility.

Every time an adult speaks "on behalf of" a certain understanding of a film that is foreign to his own strictly personal experience, and a child's understanding in particular, he runs the risk of paternalism and of intellectual dishonesty. The adult (or the educator) must evaluate the film on the basis of his own tastes, his expertise, his convictions, and his affiliations. How could he do otherwise? But it's one thing to speak from the perspective of his own experience, and another thing – much more disagreeable – to do so "on behalf" of children, even if one is speaking "for" them.

It is not unusual, however, for the teacher to exercise vigilance (must he show this film? how? what should come next?), but on what grounds? Every person – even the teacher of cinema – was once a child, and in the best of cases there remains in the adult something of the child that he once was, and whose social character has not yet run its course, or has been preserved. He will thus need to appeal to that childlike part of himself – which is an essential element of the pleasure of cinema – when he watches a film and faces the challenges of teaching it. What's more, every good film viewer – unlike the know-it-all and the smart-ass – keeps a small space within himself for the child who wants to believe and who is a little dismissive of the adult he has become. The teacher can call upon this childlike part in his intimate understanding of the film. It is always much more questionable to exercise one's judgment on a film – even one that is explicitly intended for a young audience – "on behalf of" children and their taste or their pleasure. The pedagogical superego risks suppressing what is essential, namely two truths in one's individual history that the smallest amount of self-analysis would be enough to reveal on its own: the constitution of one's own tastes and his own personal criteria in matters of aesthetic judgment.

The first truth is that the child is the most uncompromising viewer of all when it comes to the criterion of his own pleasure. No cultural intimidation or critique will ever succeed in causing him to renounce, in his heart of hearts, the pleasure or displeasure that he has genuinely felt upon viewing a film. An educator will not be able to do much to counter what, for the child, is irreducible in the lived evidence of the viewing experience. In some ways, the same is still true in adults, but in their avowed assessments of films, the latter are always, to a greater or lesser degree, social creatures, concerned with appearances and compromise. Cinema, now more than ever, has become a social medium, and every person knows nowadays that what he says about films, within his network of acquaintances, contributes to the construction of his own image. This becomes complicated when a person rejects, out of sincere preference and conviction, a "powerful" film that is perceived to be universally beloved and of-the-moment. It sometimes requires a great deal of strength to stay true to your own tastes when they come into conflict with the destructive emotional force of collective enthusiasm, and when your assessment relegates you immediately to the despised caste of heartless intellectuals, with which you, as a feeling person, naturally have no wish to be associated.

The second truth, which I'm borrowing

from a memory of Fernand Deligny, is the child's incredible and cheering capacity for digesting everything, good and bad. Any overly pedagogy-centric person is entirely ridiculous in relation to this evidence that no person can take shortcuts in passing down his own lived experience to another person, including and especially in the development of one's own personal tastes and opinions. Anyone who honestly examines what his preferences had been in his childhood and adolescence will almost certainly encounter a varied jumble of lovely things, mediocre objects, and nameless horrors. The route that one's taste formation follows is not a carefree walk in an English garden; it inevitably passes over unmentionable stretches, questionable backroads, dead ends where one comes within a hair's breadth of losing one's way. This is nothing to be ashamed of, for these risks and happenstances are the cost of becoming oneself. And we have no way of becoming ourselves without risk.

The only possible attitude, on the part of teachers, is to talk about the films they love with total honesty – with the child within themselves – on the condition that they had themselves taken a real pleasure in viewing the films, and had not merely grasped at the adulterated pleasures of a paternalistic pedagogism according to which "this is good for you, even if it is not good for me."

Pasolini, who was haunted by this question of what can and can't be passed down from one generation to the next, wrote in *Petrolio*, his last great novel, unfinished and published posthumously:

"The mystery of the life of fathers is in their existence. There are things – even the most abstract or spiritual – that are lived *only through the body*. Lived through another body, they are no longer the same.

What has been lived by the body of fathers can no longer be lived by ours. We try to reconstruct it, to imagine and interpret it; that is, we write the history of it. But ... what is most important in it inevitably escapes us.

Thus ... we cannot experience bodily the problems of boys: our body is different from theirs, and the reality experienced by their bodies is denied to us. We reconstruct it, we imagine it, we interpret it, but we do not experience it. Hence there is a mystery in the life of sons as well; and consequently there is a *continuity in the mystery* (a body that experiences reality): a continuity that breaks off with us."[29]

The adult has an obligation to preserve this mystery and to not pretend to believe that he could, with a healthy dose of goodwill, understand how adolescents experience their culture in "bodily" terms.

Another writer and filmmaker, whom you would not expect to encounter here, and who was literally obsessed with the question of transmission, was Sacha Guitry. We know how his father's artistic lineage, long denied by the elder Guitry, was a long and painful path

---

29 Pier Paolo Pasolini, *Petrolio*, trans. Ann Goldstein, New York: Pantheon Books, 1997, p. 224.

for the son. This question of transmission is at the heart of *Debureau*, a 1918 play that would be made into a film 32 years later. The famous mime of Boulevard du Temple (played by Jean-Louis Barrault in Carné's *Les Enfants du paradis*, a film that Guitry firmly disliked) forbids his son from practicing his art, and even more vehemently insists that the son not use his real name for whatever theatrical activities he engages in. "Do you believe that a person learns by studying?" he replies, when the son announces his desire to learn his father's craft. The transmission occurs, regardless, but in a mode that owes nothing to any sort of pedagogy. This relay from father to son happens all at once, in a single "lesson," before the son appears onstage to replace his dying father. Over the course of this lesson, Debureau asks his son to watch him perform pantomime, but "above all," he says, "do not copy my gestures."

Philippe Arnaud perceived in this passage a confirmation of his conviction that only desire (on the part of the student) instructs, and that "nothing is passed down according to the pedagogical pseudo-laws of a tone-deaf application of preexisting data from another's existence," or in any event nothing that is truly worth the effort: "In *Debureau*, the final performance is acknowledged as a failure, and is the first and only time that transmission occurs. More accurately, it is the brief and final touch applied to the son's old desire, the moment in which the father relents and grants his son everything – the name that he had previously denied him, the status of working as a mime, the refrain of 'You can' (much more decisive than any pre-

cise advice or performance technique) – even if all is given furtively. The whole film is a demonstration of the operating condition that is vital for any transmission: namely, the son's initial desire, for it is he, and not the teacher, who is to learn ..."[30]

The majority of great films about passing down knowledge confirm this hypothesis that "only desire instructs," and the only transmission that counts – transmission of what Blanchot calls the incommunicable – often occurs without the need for any words to be spoken, or in any case with help from very few spoken words. Perhaps not everything in a film needs to be verbalized, even in a pedagogical setting, in order for children to sense that something unspoken has nonetheless been seen, in complicity with the unspeakable. This is the process that is enacted in Hou Hsiao-hsien's *A Summer at Grandpa's* or in Bergman's *The Silence*: a child looks upon a world that has not been filtered or described by adults, a world where manifestations of evil are simply visible.

Regarding what is left unspoken in an exchange that is nonetheless effective, a friend – whose profession involves writing and speaking on the subject of cinema – recounted to me what happens when he goes to see a movie with his son. They don't speak upon exiting the film; instead, several days later, he determines whether his son enjoyed the film according to whether he asks his father to buy the video. If

30 Philippe Arnaud, *Sacha Guitry cinéaste*, ed. Yellow Now, published by the Locarno International Film Festival, 1993.

not, his son doesn't talk about the movie again, even though the two of them had silently shared the experience of watching it together, start to finish. This is an important question: what films does an adult discuss with a child, and for what films do they remain silent? Transmission does not always require silence and tacitly shared experience. For my part, where arts education is concerned, I have never been a partisan of the pedagogical injunction in favor of leaving nothing unspoken. I have always thought that it is essential, in teaching art, to respect a space for the unsaid, for the private shock, in Julien Gracq's words, that will have occasion to resonate much later, or that will become an engine of creativity, and which might be ruined by an overly strong injunction to say everything.

Cesare Pavese wrote in 1947, in the early postwar years that witnessed the birth of a "historic" generation of cinephiles in France, who would be young adults by the time of the New Wave's emergence (Skorecki, Daney, Schefer, etc.): "A work settles nothing, just as the labor of a whole generation settles nothing. Sons, and the morrow, always start afresh, lightheartedly ignoring their fathers and what has already been done. Even hatred, a revolt against the past, is more tolerable than this bland indifference. The virtue of the ancients lay in their constitution, which always looked back to the past. This is the secret of their in-

exhaustible completeness. Because the richness of a work – of a generation – is always determined by how much of the past it contains."[31]

Pavese begins to observe, in the war's immediate aftermath, that what had previously been built up between generations, even in the younger generation's revolt against or opposition to what came before, is slowly giving way to a dull indifference where nothing can grow. Each generation has always constructed a culture of its own, in order to differentiate itself – starting in adolescence – from the culture of its parents. This new culture would be alarming to parents – it was designed to alarm them – and would allow the new generation to develop its own identity. But this "new" culture did not prevent a thread from continuing to form between the parents' culture and their children. The "youths" would listen to "their" singers, to which their parents were resistant, but they would also hear singers belonging to the generation that preceded their own, and ended up integrating the latter, too, in their culture. New tastes, new colors would come along at the appointed moment, but the thread continued to grow, and parents and children would end up singing together all the same, in the car for a weekend getaway or a family road-trip. For the last decade or two, things have been changing (in France, at least), and the severing of the thread between generations has been increasingly apparent, presenting a sizable problem, and one that is newer than it would seem, for schools. The reasons for this breakage are numerous. One is the emergence

31 Cesare Pavese, *This Business of Living*, trans. A. E. Murch, New Brunswick: Transaction Publishers, 2009, p. 295–296.

of community-centered cultures that have developed as a form of resistance to objective conditions of segregation and exclusion. These cultures are becoming more and more elaborate, but are cut off, for obvious reasons, from the civil society of the majority that they want to denounce. The individualization of the means of reception and consumption (the walkman, the internet, cassette tape distribution, etc.) allows people to choose, alone or as part of a narrow group, what to consume, without having been socialized within a larger listening culture. The realization, among sellers of cultural objects, was that the (increasingly) young public was a customer base for whom it was in the sellers' interest to cultivate specific tastes and to target them as such. These are the very conditions of life, and of cultural consumption, that have played an essential role in this intergenerational rupture.

In the realm of cinema, as elsewhere, there has emerged a "youth" culture where the adults in charge of teaching cinema don't really know what to do, for they often have the feeling that these films do not concern them personally. This holds true even if they determine with perfect clarity that these films are projecting models whose effects, in terms of image, behaviors, and language, are far from insignificant, and that adults must take these effects fully into account. This is a crucial question today, even if it is less manifest, for now, in primary schools, where children still have a great capacity for welcoming films that adults place before them. Demagoguery and commerce go hand-in-hand to promote this "youth-ism,"

whose effects schools will increasingly need to contend with, without knowing how to do so within the culture of respect and tolerance that schools require.

In the series *Le Cinéma, cent ans de jeunesse* (Cinema, one hundred years young) I had the opportunity to observe in action a simple strategy that, while not a panacea, seems to me to take a fair stance with regard to this segregation between the cinematic cultures of youths and of adults. Each year, all of the classes involved – across all levels (grades one through twelve), from several regions of France and diverse social backgrounds – delve into a single topic in cinema studies (for example: "point of view," "real vs. fiction," etc.). To tackle this question, the teachers and film-industry professionals who accompanied them for this project made use of a video containing numerous film excerpts, illustrating facets of the topic at hand, drawn from the broadest cinematic heritage. These tapes, which foreshadowed for me the themed DVDs (covering the shot, the point of view, the vocabulary of cinema) from the "Eden cinéma" collection, were not targeted for a particular age range, or a particular academic setting: each teacher or participant borrows what he deems to be of value for the pedagogical reality of his own classroom. These excerpts, selected by adults, always span a broad swath of the history of film, but obviously relate to a generationally specific culture: how could it be otherwise, without demagoguery? The (good) idea occurred to certain adults, after having worked on a series of excerpts in the classroom – covering, for example, off-screen sound – to ask students to bring to class, for the next lesson, clips from "their" films that might be added to the sequence. And these same adults, in the following class session, were introduced to films of whose very existence they had not been aware, visibly belonging to a generationally specific culture; yet the excerpts, inserted into the sequence by students, showed that the class had effectively grappled with the question of off-screen sound, and the students had understood how to transpose a question about cinema presented in class onto films that were culturally outside the realm of scholarly attention. In the best cases, the fact that this "universal" question of cinematic form should still apply, in these excerpts extracted from "their" films, preserved them as the "affective property" of these children, without giving purchase to any adult voyeurism towards a culture that was not theirs.

In the field of cinema education, another "historic" question is being confronted today in France with regard to generations, this time on the side of teachers. Cinema studies courses, where they exist, as electives in high schools, for example, have been a guaranteed presence since their inception, thanks to a generation of teachers who were products of militant cinephilia, and who were largely shaped by Ciné-clubs and film journals. This generation has been single-handedly responsible for coordinating, with enthusiasm and conviction, all of the strides cinema studies have made in na-

tional education policy for over twenty years. It developed its value system during a time when it went without saying that a cinephile would have surely seen every film, and when the love of cinema was a passion for which expenditures of time and energy were no object. This "historic" cinephilia has no equivalent among younger generations, who have come of age under very different conditions in terms of access to cinema, and for whom the process of developing cinematic tastes has been influenced by television, video, and sometimes university-level coursework. The history of cinema's entry into national education policy meant that the older "historic" – and rather homogenous – generation of teachers have held, for their entire careers, the rare jobs that existed in settings that allowed courses in cinema studies. This, too, is a set of circumstances that has not been passed down from one generation to the next. When that generation retires, the teachers who will replace them to lead courses in cinema studies will not have benefited from the experience of a more direct education, and will not resemble their predecessors at all. There will inevitably be a moment of rupture, of transformation, of shifting attitudes, none of which need cause us to worry, but to which we have given too little thought and preparation. For my part, I am still sorry for the fact that, as far as national education policy is concerned, courses in cinema studies are almost exclusively reserved for the oldest students, nearing the end of their studies, whereas these courses could be an opportunity for passing down knowledge, convictions, methods, and experiences between this first generation of militant cinephiles and the young students who would take part, preparing the younger generation to be their successors, even if there still exists no formal pedagogical methodology in the field of cinema studies. The current system of merit- and seniority-based placement, which means that these courses are virtually closed off to those who most visibly have need for them, will not help bridge this generational leap.

TEACHING CINEMA AND TEACHING IN CINEMA

Teaching is one of the privileged subjects of cinema, for the simple reason that teaching often has to do with the formulation, the inscription, the circulation, and the repetition – often unconscious – of a signifier. And cinema is one of the arts that is best situated, thanks to its temporal dimension and its sonic and visual inscription, to make immediately perceptible, visible, audible, this signifier and its mode of circulation and transmission.

In *Moonfleet*, to take one of the most classic examples, transmission occurs via the Y-shaped symbol that links the young John Mohune to his ancestor Blackbeard, and that runs like a red thread through the whole film, from the signet ring to the gravestone, from the gravestone to the stone in the well. The unconscious, which is the real driving force of this transmission, operates in the form of coded signs (to say the least!), all of which take time to become legible even to the protagonists, and to the viewer who accompanies them in the progressive unfolding of the mystery. Much circulation of the manuscript will need to

occur before the poorly numbered verses of the Bible will reveal their hidden meaning. For, in reality, what remains to be deciphered behind these fanciful gothic surfaces is the unknowable itself – that is, one's paternity status, which, in some cases, can only be a matter of belief. "Is John the son of Jeremy?" The transmission that occurs between John Mohune and Jeremy Fox involves an initiation to the decoding of signs. Fox, out on the moor, deciphering with the utmost ease the secret code of the famous manuscript, which John had discovered inside Blackbeard's locket, will (reluctantly) play a role in passing down John's inheritance, where John is already his heir, his privileged initiate.

In Clint Eastwood's *A Perfect World*, it's a mere postcard that will pass between Butch the outlaw and his father, then from Butch to little Buzz, the child that he has kidnapped. This letter, arriving from Alaska, allows the son to believe that his father has not entirely abandoned him, and when Butch is dying, he gives it to Buzz, who clings to it in turn with the force of his despair: this letter, upon which the act of transmission is inscribed, has finally arrived at its destination, at the end of what was perhaps a fatal series of repeated gestures between three generations of men.

Teaching cinema has long been achieved with help from teaching *in cinema*, as a filmic subject in itself. Many great films that have inspired the love of cinema have taken as their subject the act of teaching, of passing down an inheritance (and the encounter with evil, the initial exposure to evil). We know what role *Moonfleet* played for a generation of cinephiles, who forged a lifelong connection with cinema upon viewing it. These little boys, many of whom had had their own tangles with the question of fatherhood (with fathers who were dead, absent, weak, or ineffectual), encountered in this film, like a lightning strike, a flamboyant deployment of the question that troubled them, an actual interrogation into "what is a father?" Undoubtedly, the film also spoke to them, better than any other, on the subject of their relation to the world: a child, like them, sees things that he feels certain have something to do with him, that they are vital for him, even if he is not yet able to comprehend them completely, other than intuitively, and that they constitute the part of the mystery of the adult world upon which his future hinges: sexuality, betrayal, violence, death.

Teaching, when it is not purely a function of social life, always brings into play something that eludes the simple will to teach (which, by definition, is the objective of schools) and that belongs to the unconscious circulation of a letter, a phrase, a sign, an image. It resolutely separates hardworking filmmakers, who believe only in the budget and the screenplay, from those for whom cinema is an art, who know that cinema's powers also belong to the Symbolic, the inscription of a message whose circulation cannot possibly be policed. Cinematically, this form of transmission is naturally the most interesting – and the one which leaves the most psychic traces. It has the advantage of foregrounding the limits of goodwill in matters of cinema pedagogy. There's nothing surprising in the fact that the greatest filmmakers have tackled it, with the feeling of grappling with a subject that touches on the very essence of their art. Some of these filmmakers (such as Mizoguchi) have even made this their greatest subject. I will list, in no particular order, a few of the great films in the history of cinema that approach this question of transmission cinematically: *Uwasa no onna*, *Sansho the Bailiff*, and *Tales of the Taira Clan*, by Kenji Mizogushi; *The Color of Money*, by Martin Scorsese; *Home from the Hill*, by Vincente Minnelli; *The Silence* and *Autumn Sonata*, by Ingmar Bergman; *Germany Year Zero*, by Roberto Rossellini; *Moonfleet*, by Fritz Lang; *A Perfect World*, *Unforgiven*, and *The Bridges of Madison County*, by Clint Eastwood; *Les Oliviers de la justice*, by James Blue; *Steamboat Bill, Jr.*, by Buster Keaton; *The Kid* and *Limelight*, by Charlie Chaplin; the so-called pedagogical films of Abbas Kiarostami (*Homework* and the trilogy: *Where is the Friend's Home?*, *Life, and Nothing More...*, and *Through the Olive Trees*); *The Shanghai Gesture*, by Josef von Sternberg; *A Summer at Grandpa's*, by Hou Hsiao-hsien; *Debureau* and *Mon père avait raison*, by Sacha Guitry; most of Howard Hawks's great Westerns (*Rio Bravo*, *Rio Lobo*, *El Dorado*); *L'Enfance nue*, by Maurice Pialat; *L'Enfant sauvage*, by François Truffaut. This is only a small fraction of the list that could be compiled to demonstrate that cinema – the best cinema – has been ontologically invested in the subject of teaching.

There is one other, more cultural kind of inheritance that we talk about in relation to cinema: the inheritances that pass between filmmakers belonging to different generations, and between films, whether explicitly intentional or not. These inheritances make it possible to forge connections that are sometimes entirely unexpected between films as seemingly dissimilar as *Moonfleet* and *A Perfect World*, or Chris Marker's *La Jetée* and Terry Gilliam's *Twelve Monkeys*. Modern cinema has inscribed, in some of its most beautiful films, this kind of adoption of a cinematic father by cinematic orphans in search of an inheritance: Godard and the Fritz Lang of *Contempt*; Wenders and the Nicholas Ray of *The American Friend* and *Lightning over Water*. You could trace the thread, for example, of what is passed down through the cinemas of Fritz Lang, Nicholas Ray, Godard, Wenders, and Fassbinder, and which naturally takes up the question of fathers and sons, of how they choose one another and how they write one another into their films.

V.

One Hundred Films for an Alternative Culture

A CLASSROOM DVD LIBRARY

It's as a result of this state of affairs, at once internal to the educational system and external (the current circumstances surrounding cinema and the viewer) that the strategy that I deemed to be the most appropriate and most urgent, in national education policy, was twofold: first, to furnish an initial supply of films that could constitute an alternative to purely consumerist cinema; and second, to establish and put forward, thanks to the possibilities afforded by DVD technology, a cinematic pedagogy that would be light on didacticism, essentially based on setting up connections between films, sequences, shots, and images drawn from other art forms.

In my view, the first of the two proposals is of the utmost importance. Children and young people today have fewer and fewer opportunities, in their day-to-day social lives, to encounter films outside the "mainstream" of ordinary consumption. The classroom (and the programs associated with it)[32] is the last remaining space where this encounter can still

32 I am referring here to *Ecole et cinéma*, *Collège et cinéma*, and *Lycéens au cinéma*, which for years have been working on this question of acculturation to alternative cinema.

take place. Thus it is now, more than ever before, the task of schools to facilitate access – by simple, sustainable means – to a collection of films that offer an elevated understanding, without demagogy, of the best work that cinema has produced, and an elevated understanding of all cinema.

The DVDs in the "Eden Cinema" collection share this objective of building, over a few years, an initial video library that I want to characterize as "urgent," comprising a hundred or so films, a tiny island of stability in the face of rampant amnesia and the increasingly rapid cycle of tentpole films, each of which erases the memory of the one before it, even as it more or less recycles the same poster design. A hundred films, watched and re-watched over time, to which students would continually return over the course of their education, would constitute a real salve and a significant alternative. It would not be a matter of instating a curriculum with required films, the study of which would be subjected to grading or testing; rather, the collection would resemble a treasure chest, as readily available to the teachers as to the students, liable to be summoned forth in the form of film excerpts at any moment in the life of the classroom. The magic of cinema is in its capacity to inspire spontaneously, without the help of artificial stimulants, the curiosity and desire of children, and the same is true for films that an adult would not even think to suggest to them. A teacher friend of mine works in one of the most "extreme" classrooms in France, a sort of "wild animal cage" reserved for children whom the school systems have rejected, deemed to be lost causes, violent, and incapable, early in the year, of the slightest act of concentration. He managed to capture their attention and their interest with films like Robert Bresson's *A Man Escaped*, which no one would have dared to show even to children in ordinary learning environments.

This collection must bring together films drawn from all of world cinema (from India as well as from America, from Africa and China as well as from France) and from every period of cinema's history. This is not for the sake of ecumenicalism, nor encyclopedic scope, but rather for two primary reasons.

The first reason is that the strength of cinema, and the power of the experience that the best films provide us with, resides in the fact that cinema "gives us access to experiences other than our own, allows us to share, even for just a few seconds, something very different." These words come from Serge Daney, who added, in reference to this lived, intimate experience of otherness that cinema, perhaps more intrinsically than any other art form, enables: "I am grateful to cinema for this."

When I talk of universality, I am of course not referring to the universalism that unoriginal films, made to please everybody, strive for. The universality of Hou Hsiao-hsien is the universality of being utterly Taiwanese; Mustapha Dao's is the universality of being oneself against the backdrop of the African folklore tradition. Such universality does not bear the slightest relation to these new "European" productions, which result in bland films based on a mathematical average of European culture, carefully eliminating all the eccentricities that would create difference.

The second reason is that, more and more, the cinema put forward by everyday consumption erases every trace of its own past, and of anything that is not itself. The increasingly quick succession of "must-see films" is accompanied by the erasure of all origins, all ties to the history of cinema, to which every film, like it or not, is indebted. Certain blockbusters, remakes of older films, succeed in shedding their roots by utterly ignoring them, as though they must above all else owe nothing to their predecessors. Clint Eastwood is an excellent counterexample to this desire to owe nothing to the past: each of his films leans on the great tradition of genre films in American cinema, whose heritage Eastwood takes up in order to create innovative contemporary forms.

This DVD collection must be present in a form that is not intimidating, easy to access, and permanently installed in the very structure of the classroom. Upon seeing the first titles arrive,

I dreamed of the day when two or three children, instead of going outside for recess, could freely watch, solely because they wanted to, without requiring an adult's presence, a three-minute scene from Kiarostami's *Where Is the Friend's Home?*, from Truffaut's *The 400 Blows*, from Djibril Diop Mambety's *The Little Girl Who Sold the Sun*, or from Fritz Lang's *Moonfleet*. On that day, something will have radically changed in the classroom's relationship to cinema. If, at the same time, teachers of every discipline – having gradually adapted, like their students, to this classroom (or school-wide) video library – were to begin to make use of it with the same freeness, for very diverse purposes, at every moment, and not merely during periods set aside for cinema studies, then the cinema hypothesis will have attained its full meaning.

As a result of this kind of regular, slow-and-steady attention to a hundred films – all detached from short-lived collective styles and enthusiasms – in the classroom, over the course of a child's education, through a process of slow infusion, of successive approaches from a variety of angles, in the context of different courses, there will begin to emerge the early signs of a taste for cinema that has nothing at all to do with what we still call "popular tastes," dictated by commercial supply. It is not a matter of developing a different taste, but simply of developing *a* taste; not by forcefully dealing out "value judgments" that are too concentrated to be really assimilable (like vitamin capsules that are mostly rejected by the body), but rather by way of the gradual and repeated attention to the artworks. From this point of view, a field trip to the movie theater, even when well-organized and drawn out, is not enough. In order to carry some weight in the development of taste today, it is imperative that films should also be *in* classrooms, so that cinema can become a habit by way of infusion.

The situation has changed considerably since the period during which, though films were not equal in the eyes of the public (they never were), there was much less segregation between commercial films and really creative or historically significant films. During the years of my earliest encounter with cinema, the same theaters screened the films of Cecil B. DeMille, the first films of the Nouvelle Vague, and classic French comedies. Even if advertising budgets have always been unequal, the more costly films did not fill up virtually all of the movie theaters, and all, or nearly all, of the media coverage devoted to film, as bigger films do today. Thus films are now more unequal than ever before in the eyes of the public, a fact which has the effect of sneakily edging out the films that are "different," the films that are canonical to the history of cinema, and relegating them to a ghetto that is becoming more and more closed off. Schools have a responsibility to put forward another kind of culture, one which has never claimed to be "alternative," but which will end up becoming just that, grudgingly, in the face of a version of cinema that is being imposed more and more forcefully as "the whole" of cinema. It is perhaps simply THE culture, in its entirely, that is on the verge of becoming "the exception" in relation to the huge wrecking ball of industrial production.

FROM POKEMON TO DREYER

For my part, I have never believed in the "from-Pokemon-to-Dreyer" theory, according to which educators ought to use as a point of departure what children love spontaneously, in order to lead them, little by little, toward more difficult films. In the field of literature, everyone remembers what happened in the Seventies, when humanities professors elected to start with Boris Vian, before moving progressively in the direction of Flaubert: *Madame Bovary* long awaited, in vain, these new readers, who ended up getting stuck in the pages of *L'Ecume des jours*, and taking ecstatic refuge in *Astérix*.

The argument for "starting with what they love" is often marred by demagoguery and by a certain contempt for the child. This is especially true at a time when we know perfectly well how they were led to "love what they love." We are further than ever from a spontaneous, or individual, taste or appetite, which would indeed merit consideration and respect. The disciples of the "from-Pokemon-to-Dreyer" theory act as if they don't understand that today, where cinema is concerned, the young public is first and foremost a target for marketers of films and ancillary products, who, for their part, have neither care nor respect for the formation of children's tastes.

The role of schools, with regard to an introduction to the arts, must be to provide a cultural "ski-lift" out of these pseudo-tastes created by marketing. True artistic sensitivity can only develop on the basis of an encounter with the fundamental otherness of the work of art. Only the shock and mystery that the artwork represents, in relation to the commonplace, predigested images and sounds of daily consumption, is genuinely formative. Anything else shows merely contempt toward both the art and the child. Art can be nothing but that which resists, that which is unforeseeable, that which initially throws the viewer off-balance. Art must remain, even in pedagogical contexts, an encounter that undermines all of our cultural habits. Whoever purports to steer students smoothly from consumerist products to art is already guilty of misperception and betrayal with regard to art. If a person wants to dress up culture in order to render it more appetizing or digestible, it is because he is deeply convinced that culture is a bitter pill whose flavor must be disguised. True access to art can never be comfortable or passive. One cannot "lure" children toward art like bulls to the cart. One must expose them to art, even if the engagement is sometimes explosive. It is not art that must be exposed to young viewers, risk-free, but rather the young viewers who must be exposed to art, and who might be overwhelmed in the process.

The most beautiful films to show children are not those in which the filmmaker tries to protect them from the world, but often rather those in which another child plays the role of a buffer, an intermediary, in this exposure to the world, to the evil in the world, to the incomprehensible. These are the films that have the most profound effect on children and adolescents: *The Night of the Hunter, Moonfleet, A Perfect World, A Summer at Grandpa's, Germany Year Zero*... This kind of character, with whom a viewer can identify even when the viewer understands no better than the character the evil that surrounds him (in which case the viewer identifies with his incomprehension), protects the viewer from the aggressions of the world as they are presented in the film, without hiding them. Exposure to the evil that circulates (Bresson) or that appears out of nowhere (Buñuel) in the world is less traumatizing if it passes through a fictional character who confronts it "in our place," on the front lines, in order to let us get a bit of distance and reserve. It is better to identify with a character of this sort, who does not understand everything, than to feel "directly," personally excluded from what you, the viewer, don't understand. The same holds true for the adult in a film noir: if the private detective moves through scenes without understanding them right away, we are not embarrassed to do the same, and to watch what happens to him without first seeking to get to the bottom of the meaning of the scene. This is already a pedagogy of watching: to be willing to see things, in all their mystery, before attaching words and meaning to them.

There is no path, straight or winding, that would lead from classic American films to Kiarostami's *Where Is the Friend's Home?*, Pasolini's *The Gospel According to Matthew*, or Hou Hsiao-hsien's *A Summer at Grandpa's*. There is nothing to "apologize for" in the "slowness" of the films of Abbas Kiarostami or Hou Hsiao-hsien; rather, children who are accustomed to other films, other rhythms, other stories ought to be exposed to these films calmly, without fuss. Educators must also calmly accept the first reactions, even if disagreeable, provoked in children by the shock of being confronted with a cinema of which they might not even have the slightest idea. The only real experience possible in the encounter with a work of art must include the feeling of being forced out of the comfort of one's habits of consumption and received ideas. This experience manifests itself spontaneously in initial attitudes of rejection and defiance, among children and especially among adolescents in a group, who are careful not to look foolish in front of their peers.

What speaks most forcefully to a child, as with an adult, is not necessarily what he is in the habit of hearing. The whole question is to know what we mean by "speaks to." If we restrict our meaning to the everyday content that is communicated in the media, then films are indeed "custom-made" to speak to children as a mass audience, and they speak to all children in the same manner. If we consider art to be first and foremost a personal shock, then "speaking to" is something much more intimate, uncomfortable, mysterious. This encounter is what we must aim for, even if the effects are not immediately visible or quantifiable. A real encounter with art is the encounter that leaves a lasting trace.

Alain Bergala

CINEMA, LITTLE BY LITTLE

In order to resist even the slightest bit of the amnesiac consumerism to which much of cinema is in thrall today, we must take into account the factor of time. The enthusiasm for films that one is 'socially obliged' to have seen has replaced taste, which can only be formed through the accumulation of cultural knowledge, and which requires time and memory. Taste, in any domain, can only develop slowly, little by little, step by step. It cannot be taught like a dogma. At best it is passed down, pointed out, but it must be established on the basis of repeated engagement with a collection of works which must be slowly assimilated, and must work via infusion, rather than by willful transmission. The role of primary schools, today, should initially be to facilitate the encounter with the work of art, for which the best setting is, more than ever before, the movie theater. But this encounter must be extended through a lasting engagement with the same films, where each student can tame the works little by little, incorporating them within his own imagination. It is nothing less than a cinematic imagination that must be reconstituted, where often nothing exists previously but a superimposition of self-contained, disconnected film viewings.

The encounter with film in the theater, guaranteed in programs like *Ecole et cinéma*, *Collège au cinéma*, and *Lycéens au cinéma*, is indispensable. But national education policymakers, if they truly intend to lead a movement bringing cinema into the education system, cannot be satisfied with that. What would a musical education be if it consisted of bringing children to a concert three times a year, without giving them access to recorded music? Or an education in the visual arts that was limited to museum visits, without the possibility of working on classroom reproductions of the paintings? Any serious policy of teaching cinema in schools can have no chance of being effective if there are not also films in the classroom, permanently, just as there are books and CDs.

The other key reason in favor of maintaining a film collection in the classroom is that the increasing concentration of movie theaters in France is creating "cinema deserts" where a growing number of children do not have access to any local movie theater. And if it so happens that these students occasionally go to see a film with their parents at the multiplex that adjoins the supermarket, on a big Saturday shopping trip, there is little chance that they will encounter *Where Is the Friend's Home?* or even *The 400 Blows*. For these children, the presence of a film collection in the classroom or in the school building seems to me to be virtually the duty of national education policymakers. They alone can create the conditions for contact, which might perhaps turn into an encounter, even if nothing can ever guarantee that an encounter will unfold.

Ideally, this film collection would accompany students over the course of their education, from preschool to the last years of secondary school. It was on this principle that the "Eden Cinema" collection was conceived, in its refusal to "target" a precise age range, to use an awful marketing term: each DVD is simultaneously compiled and segmented so that the same student can be introduced to one sequence in preschool, three more in first grade, the entire film in middle school, certain analyses in high school. It's not the films that will change along the way, but the approach that each student can take to them according to his level of maturity, of knowledge, of analytical ability. (None of this is to discount the fact that there obviously also exist certain masterpieces that require an adult viewer, and which would hold no interest for a child in primary or middle school.)

Cinema is also a medium of words, of dialogue, of language. With the DVD format, which can easily accommodate multiple versions of a film, there is no longer any reason to discard the version dubbed in French – which would allow a preschool or kindergarten student to access a scene from an American or Italian film – since the same child will be able to watch the same film later in its original version, with subtitles, on the same disc. He will even have access, by then, to the English or Italian-language version of the film, entirely subtitled in the original language (with each word printed in English or in Italian, as spoken, in the subtitles) as an introduction to a foreign language. We must continue to fight against the avoidance of original-language versions for films broadcast on French television, even on those channels with a cultural bent, and in the large movie theater chains, but the problem of access to different versions must be regarded differently in schools, where the DVD format

ought to be used to the best of its pedagogical potential.

IN BETWEEN THE MOVIE THEATER AND
THE INTERNET: THE DVD

Hardly more than a year has passed since the Five-Year Plan was announced, during which time there has been much controversy – at the intersection of ideology, techno-commercial evolution, and pedagogical stakes – regarding the introduction of a DVD collection in the classroom, in a broader effort to teach cinema as an art form. One year later, a symbolic blockage has visibly dissolved, and the polemics on the DVD have subsided, even if this required much patience and explication.

The announcement that DVDs would be produced for use in the classroom immediately provoked a twofold reaction, which I can summarize as follows:

On the side of movie theaters and programs created around them, there were those who responded to me that there was no salvation to be had outside the movie theater, and that DVDs in schools would precipitate the abandonment of the practice of screening films in theaters. It is true that the announcement arrived in a difficult context for independent movie theaters, whose mission is to distribute the most creative films.

On the side of techno-futurist ideology, there were those who retorted that the DVD, as a material object, already belonged to the past, and that it was absurd to select a few meagre film titles (six for the first year) when, soon, anyone would be able to summon thousands

of films at will on the Internet. This techno-futurist attitude is often, in reality, merely a manifestation of complacent do-nothingness concealed behind a jeering and arrogant eagerness
to forge ahead, which is never called upon to
furnish evidence to support its claims: "What
you are doing is already obsolete, whereas I'm
waiting for my dreamed-of future to arrive before I will begin to do anything." Since the
technological horizon is always receding, this
stance allows individuals to remain resolutely
immobile while pronouncing prophecies and
anathemas whose validity no one will be able
to verify later.

CONCERNING MOVIE THEATERS

Those who reacted strongly to the announcement that cinema studies DVDs would be produced for use in primary schools were only attending to one aspect of the news, which they
regarded as a red flag: children would be able
to watch – indeed, to "project" – films in the
classroom. The cause for alarm lay in the fact
that the classroom or the school could become
a screening space that would potentially compete with movie theaters.

The argument put forward was always the
same: the movie theater should remain the exclusive, indispensable site for collective encounters with film. Without the theater and its
collective audience, without getting distance
from the school building, without the "magic"
of projection in the dark, there could be no
benefit to the experience. One might be content to accept all of this out of pure conviction,
as a "credo" that was closed to debate. One

might also, instead, try to understand what is
meant by this reverence for the "magic" of theatrical projection, to which, incidentally, I have
always personally adhered, and which I have
never stopped defending in the course of this
brief quarrel.

After all, the argument in favor of collective
viewing is not really an argument: in what way
would a group coming together in a school
building to watch a movie be less collective
than the group coming together in a movie
theater? Institutionalized Ciné-clubs, during
the heyday of glorious 16mm projection, were
undeniably largely responsible for the value of
ritualized collective screenings and their irreplaceable effects on the viewers' reception of
a film. The argument for moving beyond the
enclosure of the school building is a double-
edged sword. It's true that students' attitudes
– and perhaps their openness to a work of art
– is doubtless not the same in the institutional
framing of the classroom, site of obligations
and assignments, and in a prestigious establish-
ment out in the world, decked out in commercial seductions. But we also know that the excitement of a school outing sometimes pro-
duces the adverse effects of distraction and
uninhibited behavior, which don't always facilitate the desired concentration on the film
itself.

Comfort is an equally dubious argument with
regard to the integration of cinema in each person's private development. How many children have fallen in love with cinema while in
the greatest discomfort – holding their breaths,

hiding behind a couch – watching bits and pieces of films that their parents, by sending them to bed, had implicitly forbidden them from seeing? The books that matter in a lifetime are sometimes the ones read in the worst conditions of discomfort. I have always liked those people who you pass in the street, their nose in the last pages of a book, oblivious to everything around them, walking to work to do who-knows-what, snatching the free moments of their day to attend to the intimate urgency of impassioned reading. I'm sure that they might not even take the same stolen pleasure in their activity if they were comfortably seated in an armchair at home, instead of in the middle of noisy traffic, on rationed time.

His name has never been mentioned, but the shadow of Walter Benjamin has, at least in my eyes, unceasingly hovered over this entire story. Ultimately, even if it has never been explicitly stated in the course of this debate, the only real difference between theatrical projection and screening a film on DVD is surely, in the final analysis, related to the Benjaminian notion of the aura.[33] There is genuinely, in the encounter with a film projected in a movie theater, something unique and irreplaceable: the presence (normally concealed from the viewers' sight) of a film reel unfurling, physical image after physical image, in a machine whose mechanical gearwheels, studded with

metal teeth, advance the film. Theatrical exhibitors are not wrong to be proud – deservedly so – of their pedagogical intervention, which consists in allowing students to visit the celebrated, mysterious projection booth, where they can see and touch this fetishized film, admire the machine that projects the images on the screen, and meet the man who enacts all of this in the shadows.

The only radical difference that really holds water, between a DVD screening in the classroom, with good projection equipment, and a screening in a movie theater, is the presence of "real," analog images, chemically inscribed on film, images that can be scratched or torn, uniquely modifying this material version of the film. Between a physical copy of a film (even if it is already, strictly speaking, a reproduction, and there exist many others) and the same film burned onto a DVD, there remains a qualitative gap, however small, of the same order as the gap that Walter Benjamin theorized between the unique work of art (and the aura attached to it) and its technological reproduction into multiple copies, all rigorously identical to one another. The digital brought about this difference: all of the DVDs engraved with the same film are rigorously the same, which was not yet entirely the case with reproductions on videocassette, and which has never been the case with film prints, which are differentiable from their first passage through a projector, and even upon removal from the chemical bath in the laboratory. The second difference is ontological: with a film print, you can cut out a single frame, hold it in your hand, and look

33 "The Work of Art in the Age of its Technological Reproducibility: Second Version" in Walter Benjamin, *The Work of Art in the Age of its Technological Reproducibility, and Other Writings*, eds. M. W. Jennings et al., Cambridge: Harvard University Press, 2008, p. 19–55.

at it directly like a slide. To borrow Roland Barthes's idea, there is no break in the continuity between the material image of Charlie Chaplin inscribed on this frame and the negative that was inside the camera on the day the film was shot. This piece of film whose image is projected on the screen in front of me was directly derived, by successive connections, to the film that captured the light reflected by Chaplin's body, which penetrated the lens to leave an impression directly on the first negative, on the day of shooting. The images projected from a videocassette had already lost this magical virtue of the analog, but the medium for these images was still a linear strip unfurling from one spool onto another. The DVD has definitively de-linearized the reproduction of the images, and this fact makes it easier to understand the fear that has taken hold of the defenders of theatrical projection. In a DVD screening, utterly nothing remains of the specificities of a cinematic screening, which is still the basis – even if its time has run out – for the famous "magic" that clings, in the end, to the aura attached to the presence – at once nearby and faraway, in the booth – of those long ribbons of celluloid.

But the major misunderstanding, in this matter, is the result of the opponents to DVDs in schools crying wolf before even having given the proposal a chance, by imagining that it would develop along the lines of what they most feared: a distribution format that would threaten to replace theatrical projection. To be clear, watching a film in its entirety, in one sitting, is the last thing for which the DVDs in this collection, designed for use in the classroom, were conceived and realized. What's more, if that had been the goal, we would have elected to use good old videocassettes, because of the current inadequacy of the DVD equipment in schools.

We were also reproached for making a "trendy" and risky technical choice in using DVDs, whose future is far from guaranteed. Today, no one can doubt that the shift away from videocassettes and toward DVDs has become irreversible, and if we are to avoid a regrettable pedagogical obsolescence, schools must take this technological development into account, for the sake of their own needs and objectives.

CONCERNING THE INTERNET

Nowadays, we frequently encounter this tendency to believe that new technologies, and especially the Internet, will soon definitively resolve all of the problems surrounding access to films. In this near-future world, every individual, wherever he is – at home, in class, at the office – will be able to instantly and precisely call up the sequence in *Rio Bravo* that begins at minute 27, or the final scene of *Through the Olive Trees*. Imagine – even if we still have a long way to go, techno-commercially speaking – the ways in which this will transform cinema education. Behaviors, at least at first, will very probably tend towards generalized channel-surfing. The classroom DVD library has the virtue of performing an initial process of selection and promotion; the complete catalogue will discourage those who don't know what they're looking for in advance. Where ought one to turn when confronted with the infinite range of possibilities made accessible by an immense catalogue where nothing (no valuation pertaining to a given value system, whatever it may be) remains to distinguish one film from another? All of these indications would raise concerns that impatience would run amok and that circulating freely in an unlimited virtual cinematheque would give free reign to distraction. One need only observe, in an environment where many "self-service" screens are present – at an education convention, for example – how children flock to this free Internet access in order to discover what the media outlets have most insistently designated as being desirable. Curiosity is more biased here than elsewhere: you log on in order to get caught up with the majority choice, the pre-selected winner, a bit like the audience for a large film distribution network who are responsible for the label affixed to certain movie posters, at the entrance to theaters: "audience favorite." In other words: we have relieved you of the task even of having to choose and to desire, since others, who are like you, have done it for you.

Simone Weil wrote that "the authentic and pure values, truth, beauty, and goodness, in the activity of a human being are the result of one and the same act, a certain application of the full attention to the object. Teaching

should have no aim but to prepare, by training the attention, for the possibility of such an act." These words are more relevant now than ever before: it has become vitally important to place children in a position to apply to a film, a work of art, the fullness of their attention, when, in today's world, there seems to be very little that calls upon them to use it. This kind of attention, as Simone Weil observes in the same chapter, "is bound up with desire. Not with the will but with desire. Or, more exactly, with consent."[34] Desire, the only force capable of driving attention – as all children experience, sometimes painfully, on a daily basis: such desire will never have the possibility of durably becoming attached to a single subject, in the infinite revolving door of possible choices, without a strong recommendation. There is unquestionably desire in the obsessive attention to computer screens, to games and web pages, but this desire is desire for movement, for speed, for perpetual change, and not desire for a subject. The task of schools is necessarily not to amplify this already irreversible development. There can be no method for teaching art that does not involve attention training. If what is being taught is truly art, such training must go against the current of the uncivilized and generalized conditioning in the direction of inattention, and must be applied to films that are singular, celebrated, physically present in the classroom, films that will continue to be objects of study. Yet making these films "desirable" is another matter altogether – the most delicate, and the hardest to institute. There can be no love of art without choice. The class-

34 Simone Weil, "Attention and Will" in *Gravity and Grace*, trans. Arthur Wills, Lincoln: University of Nebraska Press, 1997, p. 169–176.

room DVD library can modestly help with this choice.

In matters of teaching, all that really counts, symbolically, is what is pointed out. And the presence of objects that can be watched, touched, manipulated, is part of this pointing-out. It matters now more than ever, in the era of the virtual, that there are material objects in the classroom. The availability of films online will change nothing with regard to the essential question of pointing-out. You can only desire what has been pointed out: this is for you!

An introduction to art can sometimes be as simple as depositing the right object at the right moment in the presence of the right person. Walter Benjamin spoke of collectors who, "by letting you enter their homes, are not showing off their treasures. You would hardly even say they are showing them to you. They are merely allowing you to see them."

VI

Toward a Pedagogy of Fragments:
Excerpts in Conversation

The choice of the DVD format for a classroom film collection was first and foremost the result of pedagogical considerations, and not a selection based merely on modernist or technologist motivations.

The decisive technological progress encapsulated in the shift from videocassette to DVD is certainly a non-negligible advantage, but I will say that it is almost a secondary advantage. It's true that we have never, before now, enjoyed an audiovisual transmission medium of such high quality (as much for the image as for the sound), even when screened in a room with poorly shuttered windows, as is often the case in a school setting, where obtaining true darkness in classrooms is often impossible. Still, this progress, while appreciable, is, in and of itself, merely the provisional stage of a process of techno-commercial evolution that has cut the price of high-quality collective projection – in school settings – to ten or twenty times less than it was barely a decade ago, even if it is still burdensome for the budget of a primary or middle school, and will still, for some time yet, necessitate special financing.

I don't doubt that the "second blackboard" of digital projection will quickly become indispensable, independently of specifically cinematic education, but rather in all fields that

involve the examination of documents and data, and dialogue between interconnected courses. It presents a decisive pedagogical advantage, compared to individual screens: everyone can follow an Internet search at the same time, guided by the instructor or by a student, and can learn together to overcome the challenge of not getting lost and arriving at the appointed goal.

The real innovation of the DVD in cinema education, however, operates on another level: this new format makes possible the conception and implementation of new forms of pedagogy, which were previously impractical due to the linear mode of consumption inherent to the videocassette. Not every technological innovation necessarily opens new pedagogical horizons. Certain innovations merely contribute to the general improvement of the conditions of pedagogical practice, without transforming them. There was something worth taking advantage of, for the sake of providing an introduction to cinema, in the possibilities that DVD offered, for rethinking new pedagogical forms that move beyond the proven limitations of videocassettes.

Cinema-based pedagogical tools have long been rooted in a dominant, and antiquated, didactic model: that of the voiceover commentary that knows, decodes, analyzes, comments on shots and sequences in a film. When a teacher of cinema studies plays this kind of tape, referred to as film analytic video, in class, he is handing over the floor to a recognized expert who is fluent in the specific content (this or that film, one or another auteur), and who is well-acquainted with all the methods of film analysis. This supposedly all-knowing voice delivers the results of a thought process and an analysis for which the baseline assumptions, the genesis, the mechanisms are beyond us. Most often, this discourse involves drawing on visual and auditory "evidence," in the form of shots, frozen images, and film clips, all carefully assembled. I have always thought that we ought to be wary of such evidence the moment it is invoked by someone clever, who could just as easily bring his audience to subscribe to a fallacious discourse. It would not be very difficult, by shrewdly selecting certain shots and certain edits in Godard's *Breathless*, for example, to demonstrate an absolute untruth – asserting, for instance, that the film scrupulously respects the rules of classical montage, and giving visible evidence in support of the assertion.

This form of didacticism (analytic or demonstrative discourse that places a heavy burden on images) is derived from a mode of knowledge transmission whose merits and efficacy are still indisputable, and it would be pointless and absurd to deprive oneself of its benefits. There are still lovely analytic videos to be made that will satisfy certain needs in the domain of cinema education. There's no doubt that people will continue to resort to this kind of pedagogy for a long time – a pedagogy that is vertical (passing from he who knows to he who is learning) and linear (with discourse unfolding as in a lecture or classroom lesson), and which has long been the mode of the videocassette. But now, it is possible to invent other pedagogies.

In the field of cinema studies education, DVD technology is currently ushering in the new possibility of a pedagogy structured around relationships between films or film fragments placed in dialogue, a pedagogy light on didacticism, where discourse is no longer the bearer of knowledge, but where ideas are born from simply observing these varied relationships and the flow of fragments.

The novelty of the DVD – in relation to older film distribution formats – resides strictly in the fact that it is possible to instantly access (without the need for tedious and unpredictable rewinding) any given precise fragment of a film, and just as instantaneously to place it in dialogue with other images and other sounds: another clip from the same film, a segment from another film, the reproduction of a painting, the director's audio commentary, an archival document, and so on. It's true that CD-rom technology has already long enabled this kind of rapid flow and relationship-building, but with regard to cinema specifically, the CD-rom's storage capacity, its digital format, and its quality of reproduction were clearly insufficient for a collective pedagogical application.

It's in this capacity – the ease of calling up fragments and placing them in dialogue – that makes the DVD a precious tool for the possibilities for pedagogical innovation that it offers.

The DVD really makes possible what Nabokov desired for novel readers: the ability to access instantaneously, at the same time, both the whole work and its detailed elements; to compare two details separated by time or space; to wander freely in the film "as in a painting"; in short, to have access to a new way of approaching the film, a tabular approach in addition to the traditional linear mode of consumption.

The DVD makes it possible to store up a great number of images and sounds, and to arrange, by very simple means, multiple "strings" that offer as many ways of associating these cinematic fragments in relationships that "think," and that enable students to think about cinema.

We were already able to record multiple sequences together on a videocassette, but such recordings imposed an immovable ordering and inflexible juxtapositions. On a standard DVD, thirty excerpts can be placed in dialogue with one another according to predetermined chains where each clip finds itself caught up in multiple relationships and linkages. Today, with this new tool, it is important to have a precise and rigorous theory of this kind of relationship-making between film clips. This could be one of the centerpieces (for there will certainly be others) of a pedagogy that appeals to the imagination and the personal intelligence of the user, whether student or teacher. The short form, whether of an excerpt or a sequence, combines the merits of quick thinking (comparing three clips sometimes provides a greater depth of understanding than one long discussion) and a cross-sectional perspective (you can discover unexpected, enlightening, and exciting relationships between cinematic traditions, films, and auteurs, that a more linear approach would have kept distinct, relegated to airtight categories).

Incidentally, I am insistent on the fact that the instantaneous juxtaposition of excerpts, and the speed of accessing and moving through them, are not developments that align with the generalized impatience that is often associated with channel- and web-surfing. There is no reason not to make use of this digital speed, but only for purposes of "dynamic juxtaposition," of inciting thought. This is especially true inasmuch as the DVD also facilitates, with great visual quality, the inverse action – indispensable in educational contexts – of slowing down and stopping the flow of images.

Under these conditions, the teacher and the students together can observe, ponder, and dissect the idea or concept that each linkage implicitly brings into play. Intelligence is not necessarily the result of one supposedly authoritative voice or text, nor is it the exclusive domain of experts; rather, it is in the movement between film excerpts itself, which is sufficient, under certain conditions of observation and attention, to provide food for thought. It is undoubtedly one possible opening by which to escape didacticism. It's possible to imagine different strategies for using these E.I.C.s – "excerpts in conversation" – depending on the intended audience, ranging from the most playful to the most conceptual, from the poetic to the linguistic.

These ideas, inscribed in the cumulative linkages of film excerpts, do not necessarily obey the logic of the branching tree structure that is dominant in informatics theory. Our model can choose to follow more rhizomatic pathways, where the suggested chains do not necessarily present a choice that is binary or vertically hierarchical. In a collection of excerpts, one can imagine multiple flows appealing to different forms of intelligence. This opens up a corresponding multiplicity of pathways – free, non-hierarchical, setting up comparisons of all kinds (analytic, poetic, content-based, formal) between excerpts.

As a pedagogical tool, the DVD is still an artifact, conceptualized by someone who knows, and who has designed, these pathways. It nevertheless comes much closer to the nature of its object (cinema as an art form) and its functionality (spawning multiple pathways in the mind of the viewer over the course of a film) than the majority of tools that preceded it.

IN PRAISE OF THE FILM EXCERPT

I crossed paths with a young girl who knew *Pierrot le fou* by heart at the age of five, and not because her parents had shown it to her in some kind of absurd proselytism, but by having seen it in snippets, obliquely, on several occasions, while her father was watching it on his own, and by returning to it dozens of times, piecewise, as a child returns to a "racy" book, until she knew it by heart. It's not entirely an accident that this film, which no one would have dreamed of showing to a child, gripped her. It lends itself perfectly to a "piecewise" approach, experienced in bits that are easily engrained in memory: bits of dialogue ("my lifeline; ordinary and extraordinary; what can I do, I don't know what to do, do you love me") and bits of cinema (the car that throws itself into the sea with its two passengers; the couple who emerge from the sand; Belmondo waiting until the last moment to leave the train tracks where he's seated, just before the train enters the frame; the gas station gag, imitating Laurel and Hardy; inserted images from *Pieds Nickelés*; the car being set on fire; and so on). All children have the capacity and the desire to latch onto "bits" and to memorize them; I don't know why adults deprive them of the opportunity to do so, in the name of respecting the wholeness of the film. The time for wholeness will come later, much later in the case of certain films. This is why we made the choice to offer access starting in nursery school, for example, to a scene from *Au hasard Balthazar*,[35] sublime in its simplicity, where the donkey, who has just been taken in by a circus, is confronted with the gaze of other animals that he has never

---

35 This excerpt can be found on the DVD *Petit à petit le cinéma I*, along with other clips that are as far removed from the received idea of which kind of cinema ought to be viewed by children—such as Jonas Mekas's *Notes on the Circus* or Artavazd Pelechian's *Four Seasons*.

encountered in his lifetime as a donkey: a bear, a monkey, an elephant, a tiger. A four-year-old child could be touched by this scene, where cinema gives us an utterly sensitive idea of what an animal's gaze might be when exempted from all human presence, and the same child could have much to say about it. Why should we deprive him of this experience under the pretext that the film demands to be watched in its entirety by an adult viewer? If the child can fully experience three minutes of the film at an early age, we might as well offer him the opportunity instead of waiting until he's eighteen to let him see and understand the entire film – especially if this scene is not presented to him in isolation, but rather in an illuminating dialogue with other scenes from other films. With a small child who could take pleasure and interest in Papageno's melody from Mozart's *Magic Flute*, why would we offer "children's music" instead of this piece, under the pretext that he must wait at least another fifteen years to experience the opera in its entirety?

There are two ways of choosing and thinking about a film excerpt. The first involves treating it as an autonomous piece that can be received "in itself" as a small totality, without experiencing the absence of its original context. The second, on the contrary, involves treating it as a piece arbitrarily cut out of a film, where the gesture of extraction can be felt as a cross-sectioning, a suspension, a light frustration.

Both kinds of excerpts have pedagogical virtues. The first can be seen as "scale models,"

easier to hold in one's gaze than an entire film. The second represents *teasers*, playing on one's desire to see the entire film. Anyone who remembers an old television program, "La séquence du spectateur," will understand what I'm speaking of. This show aired every Sunday at noon, if memory serves me correctly, offering a simple back-to-back series of four or five film excerpts, without commentary, with nothing connecting them, and not necessarily contemporary nor even recent. It was like jabbing a probe into an anonymous person's memories of cinema. The show, simple as a butter knife, did much more to stoke several generations' desire for films than all of the other standard devices: movie trailers, posters, press coverage. The excerpted films were most often films that had had popular success, but at a time when the directors of small French films did not yet see themselves as auteurs nor as businessmen. Every Sunday the show aroused a delicious feeling of disappointment each time that the editor's blade came down to end an excerpt, and provoked a furious desire to see the film in its entirety. It produced an absolutely unpredictable montage effect, and I am surely not the only person who remembers the very particular emotion that one felt, at the moment of severance, upon extracting oneself from the universe of the film whose excerpt had just ended, and entering almost immediately into another climate, another atmosphere, belonging to the following film.

I have always been struck by the impact of the excerpt (analyzing a scene, a shot) in scholarly approaches to film. The pedagogy of the fragment often combines the merits of synthesis, freshness, and an inscription that is more precise and more durable than the images that reside in memory. Entering in the middle a film that one has already seen, even knows by heart, always gives rise to moments of surprise and amazement: how have I never noticed this shot, or the strangeness of the actor's gesture here, or this lighting that has no equivalent anywhere else in the film? Because it was swept up in the stream of images from throughout the film that had already accumulated in my memory, and its roughness, its singularity, was a bit smoothed over, flattened, in viewing the whole. To see a film fragment, detached from the narrative flow and from the visual habituation that it engenders, renders the fragment newly visible. One can imagine, contrary to the habits of classical pedagogy, beginning with the study of fragments before viewing entire films. A person can fall in love with a film on the basis of a glimpsed fragment, and the desire can be keener if the film object is not handed over right away as a totality to be skimmed. Viewing a film slantwise, anamorphically, is often the mode that is most certain to incite desire. Approaching a film by way of a fragment is one of the possible forms such anamorphosis can take.

Pasolini recalled his dazzling encounter with a master who was none other than Roberto Longhi. The meeting occurred around 1939 at the University of Bologna, "in a small, out-of-the-way, hard-to-find room," where the young Pasolini, having recently arrived from his native Frioul, came across Longhi's art history course, which he, in "the infinite timidity of (his) seventeen years," regarded as "a desert island, at the heart of a starless night." Longhi, as it happens, would project slides showing details from paintings in order to draw comparisons between forms: "… a 'shot' representing a sample of the Pasolinian world … dramatically 'contradicted' a shot representing, in turn, a sample of Masaccio's world. The cloak of one Virgin contradicted the cloak of another Virgin …The close-up of one saint or attendant contradicted the close-up of another saint or another attendant … One part of the formal world was thus opposed physically, materially, to one part of another formal world: one 'form' to another 'form.'"[36] In another magnificent text, undoubtedly one of the most beautiful ever written on the revelatory role that an ingenious teacher can play in shaping the destiny of a very young man, Pasolini wrote: "For a young boy who has been stifled and humiliated by academic culture, by the conformism of fascist society, this was a revolution. He began to stumble forward in the teacher's wake. The erudition that the teacher revealed and symbolized suggested a new path in relation to the entirety of reality as he had previously known it."[37]

36 Pier Paolo Pasolini, *Ecrits sur la peinture*, coll. Arts et esthétique, ed. Carré, 1997.
37 Ibid.

Pasolini, still writing on the subject of slant-wise, partial viewing, believed that the evocative power of paintings, in the writings of Roberto Longhi, arose precisely from the fact that he always looked upon the works he was describing from a "foreshortened" perspective, anamorphosized by this uncommon point of view, which rendered the works newly visible, as though one had never seen them before. "All of Longhi's descriptions of the paintings he examined (and these were naturally the most important moments in his 'prose') are written from a foreshortened angle. Even the simplest, most direct, fully frontal painting, once 'translated' in Longhi's prose, is seen as though obliquely, from an unusual and difficult point of view." I like the last word: to "truly" see is often to see slantwise, but this kind of vision must first be "difficult," that is, must displace the habitual point of view, must resist, in order to be truly profitable.

One way of "displacing the point of view" might consist, on a DVD (whose technology has finally made it possible to instantaneously perform this operation!), in placing side by side a sequence from one film and a sequence from another film, especially if there is a great aesthetic and historical distance between the two. The perceptual and mental gymnastics required to move from one perspective to the other – from a shot by Chaplin to a shot by Peleshian, for example – means that each shot skews the other, in a way, and makes it more "visible" than it would have been in the continuity and the dominant perspectival logic of its own film.

I have long campaigned for an educational approach to cinema that takes as its starting point the shot, regarding it as the smallest living cell – animated, endowed with temporality, with a future tense, with rhythm, enjoying a relative autonomy – constitutive of the great cinematic body.

On the side of the cinematic act, the shot brings into play, in a magnificently inextricable manner, most of the choices that crop up, actually and simultaneously, during the process of cinematic creation: where to begin and where to end the shot, where to place the camera, how to organize or frame the elements that will be flowing across it. What limits ought one to place on one's own power to manipulate the objects and the world caught on film? What does one have the right to capture on film or stage for the camera? How should one incorporate the actor? How can one give him a rhythm of his own?

On the side of the viewer, the meticulous and speculative observation of a shot from a film makes it possible to pose fundamental questions about cinema: What is a shot? How did this or that great filmmaker make use of the shot in a personal way? How has the concept of the shot evolved over time, and under the influence of the great metal blades that have renewed cinema here and there? How do these shots speak to us today? How are they inhabited by the actors? What can they tell us about what the world was like, and what cinema was like, in a given year and a given country?

A well-chosen shot can be enough to demonstrate simultaneously the art of a filmmaker and of a moment in the history of cinema, insofar as it carries at once a linguistic framework, an aesthetic (necessarily inscribed in an era), but also a style, the singular mark of its auteur.

The shot, finally, as the most concrete unit of film, is the ideal interface between an analytic approach (one can observe, in even the smallest of fragments, many of cinema's linguistic parameters and elements) and an introduction to the creative act (building on a new awareness of all the choices involved in "making a shot").

VII.

Toward a "Creative Analysis"

A pedagogy of cinema stumbles most frequently over the manner in which it captures its subject. It is much more important, when faced with a complicated, lively, and unruly subject, to have the correct *attitude* than to take a risk on the comforting reassurance of knowledge. It's always better to have a teacher who knows little, but whose approach to cinema is open, without betraying its real nature, rather than a teacher who clings to a few scraps of rigid knowledge and who begins by giving the definitions of camera movements and types of shots, as though the filmmaker's first step is to think in words about choices, whereas in reality these words merely translate those choices, and are of utterly no help during the creative process.

I will now attempt to open several avenues for getting to the essence of the matter – that is to say, the reality of the cinematic creative process – by teasing out a few essential points, some of which are rarely, or badly, interrogated, and which are often at the root of the challenges encountered in education: the fundamental components of the gesture of cinematic creation

(choice, placement, approach), the real conditions under which the filmmaker makes decisions, the crucial question of the totality and the fragment, the question of the encounter between the "game-plan" and the reality of the shoot, and ultimately the question of the negative forces at work in the act of creation. With a clearer awareness of what's at stake in the cinematic gesture, on these five levels, a great deal of pedagogical fear and rigidity might vanish, and cinema education will reap the benefits.

A pedagogy of creation can begin with action, in the earliest stages of an introduction to cinema studies. There is another way of watching films, of talking about them, of analyzing them, which is the same mode of viewing that Jean Renoir demanded of his viewer: "in order to love a painting, one must be a would-be painter, or else you cannot really love it. And to love a film, one must be a would-be filmmaker. You have to be able to say to yourself, 'I would have done it this way, I would have done it that way.' You have to make films yourself, if only in your mind, but you have to make them. If not, you're not worthy of going to the movies."[38]

This radical declaration should serve as the basis for a different way of watching and ana-

38 Jean Renoir, *Renoir on Renoir: Interviews, Essays, and Remarks*, trans. Carol Voker, Cambridge: Cambridge University Press, 1989, p. 24.

lyzing films, one which would somewhat disobey the first rule of film analysis, in the "scientific" tradition of university cinema studies: namely, that analysis must be rooted in what is onscreen, and only what is onscreen. I have always pleaded for a different approach to films, an approach that I have tested for years, at the university level, in the context of a seminar dedicated to the cinematic act of creation. There is a mode of seeing and reflecting on films that would constitute a first initiation into the creative act. We could call it "creative analysis." It can be distinguished from classical film analysis in the same way that "didactic analysis," in psychoanalysis, is distinguished from therapeutic analysis, in that its aim is not only the subject's recovery, but also to create an opening for future analytic practice. "Creative analysis," unlike classical film analysis – whose only purpose is to understand, to decode, to "read the film," as they say in schools – would prepare students for, or initiate them into, creative practice. In both cases, didactic analysis and creative analysis, analysis has a transitive nature that makes it different from classical analysis. The analysis is not an end in itself, but a movement toward something else.

In this pedagogy of creation, the task at hand is to return, in one's imagination, to the moment that slightly preceded the moment of definitive inscription, where the various choices that simultaneously confronted the filmmaker were *about to be* decided, to that final moment where the possibilities were still available, to that instant, still vibrating with uncer-

tainty, of which Georges Bataille writes in his essay on Manet: "We admire one of his pictures as it hangs on the wall, but it is something else again to imagine that picture as it first existed, hovering between the uncertainty it was for the painter and the certainty it is for us. ... If we do not view these highly varied paintings in the original light in which they came into being, how mistaken we may be about them!"[39] Such could be the watchword of a pedagogy of creation: to consider these cinematic "canvases" back in the dubious and uncertain context of their origins, at the most vivid peak of the cinematic process.

It's a matter of making the logical and imaginative effort necessary to move slightly back upstream in the creative process, to the moment where the filmmaker made his decisions, where the choices were still available. This is a posture that requires practice if one is to enter into the creative process in order to understand, not how the official choice functions in the film, but how this choice presented itself to the filmmaker among many other possible choices. At every moment in cinematic creation, the filmmaker is confronted with a great number of choices, and the decision occurs at the precise instant where, between all these possibilities, he settles on a definitive choice, which he then inscribes on some medium: a painter's canvas, a blank page, a film strip or digital tape.

39 Georges Bataille, *Manet*, trans. Austryn Wainhouse and James Emmons, New York: Rizzoli International Publications, 1983, p. 99–100.

The viewer watching something on a screen will find it difficult to imagine that there might have been something different than what he's seeing, which imposes itself with the self-evidence of objects in the real world, even if he knows perfectly well that its production involved a mise-en-scène, a transformation of the real. In literature, it's easier to imagine that before words were selected and lined up by the author, there was nothing but the white page – or, in painting, the blank canvas – for the simple reason that everyone has at one time found themselves facing a blank page to be filled with words, and that everyone has at some point hesitated between several words that could have occupied the same place in a sentence. In the tradition of literary education, students learn that the studied author chose a given adjective among others from which a paradigm can be identified. Alas, in pedagogy we often also conclude that he chose the only "good" adjective possible, since he's a great writer. In reality, of course, for the writer, the actual creative process does not derive from the deployment, even mentally, of a thesaurus; yet even so, the idea persists, in reading, that there were other possibilities in addition to what was ultimately selected. In cinema, we must make a much greater – even an "unnatural" – effort of imagination, in order to conceive of everything that was still possible prior to the moment of decision, none of which can be reduced to an encoded and easily recuperable paradigm of the kind that can exist between synonyms for a word. Instead of *this* bouquet of flowers, unique and self-evident, there could have been

a thousand others, just as real and self-evident in the image. We must imagine that there might have been tulips or lilies where we now see roses.

In cinema, one always has the impression – regardless of one's knowledge on the subject – that before filming, somehow, the objects to be filmed were already there in the world, waiting to be filmed. In film theory, there is a scholarly word that conveys just this idea: "profilmic." In painting, one does not say that the landscape or the model was "propictorial," as it's so obvious that there is a radical transposition between the reality of the objects and the strokes of paint on the canvas. The language of cinema has until now been, to borrow Pasolini's definition, "the written language of reality," if we set aside animation, which clearly derives from the pictorial transposition of reality and presents itself as such. A new order is on its way, with new kinds of images that are entirely fabricated on a computer, and that enable the creation of a strong illusion of reality, while soon they will be able to do entirely without any encounter with reality.

This illusion of reality, based on a mechanical-optical recording of reality (whether the reality of a natural setting or the reality of nature reconstructed in a studio makes no difference) has always been an essential component of the pleasure of film, and even the most critical of critics and the most semiological of semiologists will not be able to hold back on this "suspension of disbelief" if they want to immerse themselves even slightly in the film and to take pleasure in it. One must first be a good viewer, willing to be duped by the illusion of reality, if one wants to have any chance, later, of being a good critic or a good analyst. Among children, this belief in the reality of the filmed reality is even more stubborn than it is among adults, and anyone who has ever endeavored to analyze a scene with young children has experienced the difficulty of getting them to admit (which obviously feels unnatural in relation to their pleasure as viewers, to which they fiercely cling) that the scene was quite simply made up of mise-en-scène, the cutting-up of shots, the choice of points of view. The other youthful pleasure of "breaking the toy" to see what's inside it, but also to appropriate it differently, will only arrive belatedly with regard to cinema, where children are more determined than in other realms to preserve their state of belief. But very quickly, with a bit of practice, the pleasure of understanding participates in the pleasure of film, which it can only amplify, contrary to the belief of those who hold old obscurantist ideas on the subject. The pleasure of understanding is as emotional and gratifying as the supposedly "innocent" pleasure of pure consumption.

Paul Valéry wrote: "... he who has not contemplated, in the blankness of his paper, an image troubled by the possible, and by regret for all the words that will not be chosen, nor seen in the limpid air a building that is not there ..., he cannot know, regardless of his expertise, the richness and the resources and the spiritual reach that are illuminated by the conscious act of constructing."[40] "Constructing,"

here, is tantamount to "creating," and not merely to the specific stage of "construction," of structure-building, that occurs in every act of creation. The phrase "regardless of his expertise" effectively makes the distinction between what can be taught by "expertise" and what can never be known by anyone, even the most learned among us, if they have not had the experience of the possibilities that are still open, the signs not yet chosen, and instead stick to the signs that have been written, confirmed, already chosen.

CHOICE / PLACEMENT / APPROACH [41]

Perhaps it would be good, in a pedagogy of creation, to contemplate the act of cinematic creation in its fundamental mental operations before considering its technical operations. Things would perhaps become clearer and simpler. Leonardo da Vinci said that painting – the most concrete of the arts, made from pigments that one deposits with a stroke of the hand, thus with one's body, on a canvas that is utterly material – is a *cosa mentale*, a mental thing. Creation, in cinema as elsewhere, is first of all a "cosa mentale" before becoming a set of concrete operations, before confronting the real, even if the real, in cinema more than in any other art, always has its say.

The sequence of operations that result in an act of creation, in cinema, is long and varied:

40 Paul Valéry, *Introduction à la méthode de Léonard de Vinci*, Folio essais, ed. Gallimard, 1992.
41 Editor's Note: Bergala's original term here is "attaque". For clarity's sake it has been translated as "approach", thus losing some of its decisive manner in relation to the idea of tackling an artistic problem.

screenwriting, casting, location scouting, shooting, editing image and sound, sound mixing, grading. From the start, this sequence seems much more heterogeneous and temporally segmented than those in the neighboring realms of creation, such as writing novels or painting. It involves worksites, machinery, concrete actions and different technical collaborators. It is often the case that certain creative collaborators never cross paths if their interventions occur at moments in the sequence that are far apart: the film editor won't necessarily meet the cameraman whose images she is editing. But with regard to what is essential – that is, the act of creation as a "cosa mentale" – this heterogeneity is perhaps deceptive.

The act of cinematic creation implements three simple mental operations: *choice, placement,* and *approach.*

This trinity seems to me to be specific to the very act of making a film, independently of the technical differentiation of this act into distinct phases. These three mental operations do not correspond to specific or chronological moments in the sequence, but rather occur simultaneously at every moment in the sequence.

In cinema, in the course of the different phases of work, it is always necessary to:
- *Choose*: to select objects in reality, from among other possibilities. While shooting: choice of settings, actors, colors, movements, rhythms. While editing: choice of takes. While mixing: choice of isolated and ambient sounds.
- *Place*: to position objects in relation to one

another. While shooting: placement of actors, elements of decor, props, extras, and so on. While editing: determining the relative order of shots. While mixing: placement of ambient and isolated sounds in relation to images.
- *Approach*: to decide on the angle or viewpoint on objects that one has chosen and placed. While shooting: determining the camera's angle of attack (in terms of distance, axis, height, lens) and that of the microphone(s). While editing: determining the opening and closing cuts, once the shots have been chosen and placed. While mixing: determining the same factors for sound.

In filming, there are typically two sorts of filmmakers. The first are those who are preoccupied, first and foremost, with the placement of their actors in space, and for whom the question of the camera's approach is wholly subordinated to this initial placement. These are filmmakers who generally will not choose the framing of a shot, or even the camera's axis or the timing of each cut, until after they have first arranged the complete space of the scene, the movements of their actors and their sets, a bit like in a theater rehearsal. The others, on the contrary, first decide on their approach (this camera axis, that framing) and then position their actors and sets as a function of this initial desire to approach the scene in this particular way, or a preference for a precise shot.

That being said, while these categories are useful for distinguishing between two major tendencies or families of cinematic creators, it goes without saying that in the act of concretely composing a shot, every filmmaker oscillates endlessly between a demand for placement and an urge towards a specific approach, a creative contradiction for which the realized, concretized shot is the dialectically enacted resolution. Real space always imposes its constraints on placement, even for the most conceptually image-oriented filmmakers, and the choice of an approach always involves revising the chosen placement, even for the filmmakers who are most respectful of the space of reference. It's often from tensions of this kind that the most lively, and vibrant, shots in cinema are born. Shots that are sensibly arranged, without these creative contradictions at work, are very much at risk of letting all life escape from their too-loose stitches.

These three fundamental mental operations – *choice, placement, approach* – are formulated here one after another, in a distinct and chronological series, merely for the sake of clarity. In the reality of cinematic practice, they are tangled in a much more dialectical way, at all stages of production. It is very rare that there is not interference and overlapping between them. A problem or approach might require one to revisit a placement choice: now that the camera is in place, for example, a masking problem has emerged that will perhaps be resolved by changing the arrangement of the actors on the set. A placement problem might require revisiting a choice of props: now that everything is situated in space, and the camera is positioned, one must perhaps recon-sider the choice of this bouquet of flowers, which attracts too much attention between the two actors, and choose instead another, more modest bouquet. The same occurs in editing: an editor might first have assembled the shots in one order, 1-2-3. Then he ultimately decides to place shot 3 in the middle, and it might turn out that the take selected for shot 3 is no longer the best choice for this new placement: he must go back to the previous step in order to choose a different take that he had rejected. This is one of the reasons why "rushes," where you choose which takes to use before knowing where they will be placed in editing, and without knowing what the adjoining shots will be, are always a little dangerous: even an accidental take near the end could reveal itself to be the best in the game, if you decide at some point to insert an elliptical edit and only use one part of the shot.

The thing that simultaneously accounts for the specificity, the difficulty, and the excitement of cinema is the fact that its mental operations, without which there can be no creation, are never purely abstract or intellectual choices that could find their validation in a pure paradise of ideas. They are necessarily in negotiation with rugged reality, through trial and error, regression, repentance, until it can be said that an equilibrium has been reached, which will not betray all of the initial idea or desire, even if one has been forced to move quite far from it due to "circumstances."

It was with regard to the apparently banal question of "point of view" that I was made aware, for the first time, of a limitation of classical analysis of the "scientific" type taught at the university level. Invited to take the floor in a training session on the question of cinematic "point of view," I embarked on a painstaking quest, in universities, for the theoretical literature that had been produced on the subject. I gathered, from reading these texts, that something was escaping the pure analyst – something which is self-evident to anyone who has had a concrete experience of mise-en-scène and of the real processes that contribute to the final "point of view" inscribed in a shot. Obviously, what we see onscreen does not derive, as the analyst postulates with a great deal of naiveté – the angelic dupe, in this instance, of the illusion of reality that he knows perfectly well how to analyze elsewhere – from a unique decision along the lines of "choosing a point of view" for a photographer who can only choose his position and his focal length when facing a given reality, in which he has no means nor any desire to directly intervene. Such would be, let's say, Cartier-Bresson's point of view while working in the street. The fiction filmmaker knows that things don't work that way, even when shooting on location in a real-world setting. The commonplace but massive feeling that the viewer gets from the point of view of a shot that he is in the process of watching (I am seeing this scene from the point of view

of…) is in fact the result of a complex dialectic between two gestures that are the daily work of the director: placement and approach.

Let us imagine a banal scene in which a couple is eating in a restaurant – a frequent cinematic occurrence. The director will perhaps begin by choosing a table for two, having found one in the reality of this restaurant. He will first need to position the man and the woman and come up with a layout, as it were, for the table: the man here, the woman there. Perhaps he will then find an initial placement for his camera – let's say, for example, behind the woman (in order to film the back of her neck), but slightly to the side so that the man's face is visible.[42] It is rare that the process ends there, even for filmmakers who are reputed to be very respectful of the real, like Rivette or Rohmer. Often something will invalidate this initial choice – for instance, a mirror where a bit of the street is reflected, and where the filmmaker is unable to control the light. The filmmaker can then decide to move the table to the right by a meter, and to move the chairs laterally, between candelabras, and no longer in line with one another. Or he realizes, looking at his framing, that in fact he would do better to film the woman from the front, listening, and the man from behind, even if he had anticipated doing the opposite on paper. He can, at this point, ask the actor and actress to switch places. The final point of view will be the result of all these successive changes to placement and approach.

42 One might recall Godard, in one of several Parisian cafés in *Vivre sa vie*, playing with the vicariousness of this point of view and the reputedly "forbidden" masking that he highlights in passing, pausing the tracking shot for an instant.

A simple example will now allow for a better understanding of what I mean by "creative analysis." Let's look at the sequence in the Roman apartment from *Contempt*. For the classical analyst, the analysis of point of view would be rather simple: it would consist in analyzing, from the appointed scenes, inasmuch as Godard rendered them definitive "by chance," the point of view chosen by Godard in shot after shot (in front of the sofa; behind Brigitte Bardot in the process of leafing through the book of erotic Roman paintings) and, perhaps, teasing out an overall structure that would allow the analyst to model the question of point of view across the entire scene.

Before Godard staged the shots that make up this long sequence of *Contempt*, there was nothing in this apartment, which was then under construction: no furniture, no color, no actors, no dolly tracks. There was a written dialogue between a man and a woman, and an empty apartment that was as white as a blank page or canvas. Godard found the apartment, with its rooms, its doors, its windows, but he had to decide on all the rest. The sofa: its color and its placement. The little coffee table, with its lamp and accompanying lamp-shade. The room that would be the bedroom, the placement of the bed in this room, the bed itself. Bardot's dressing gown and Piccoli's suit. He had to assign a location for every part of the scene: this line of dialogue in the bathroom, that other one around the coffee table, this other one in the bedroom. He had to decide, for each part, the axis and placement of the camera, whether to segment the action into two or three shots, or whether to use a panoramic or tracking shot.

There are simple strategies for helping the viewer to adopt this "creative" posture. I strongly believe, on the basis of past experimentation, in the strategy that involves bringing students back – even if, naturally, it's only via simulation – to the moment where the filmmaker had, on the one hand, his written "plan," his scenic outline in his head and on paper, and on the other hand the reality of the set where he would need to inscribe his plan; back to the moment, if you will, where Godard arrived in the empty Roman apartment that he had chosen in order to film the long domestic scene in *Contempt*. At the university level, I eventually provided students with a floor-plan of this apartment (without including any furniture or accessories) and the written dialogue of the scene, giving them time to imagine how they would tackle the mise-en-scène of this sequence, in the larger sense of the term, taking into account the three basic components of every act of direction: choice, placement, and approach.

With children, of course, you'll start with shorter scenes where they can appreciate what's essentially at stake. Take the scene in *Where Is the Friend's Home?*, for example, where the boy tries to negotiate with his mother for permission to return his friend's school note-book, which he had taken by mistake, and which is posing a grave moral dilemma for him: if his friend shows up in class the next morning without his notebook, he will be dismissed from school. Even if it refers to several specific cultural elements (the courtyard as a living space, for example), this scene offers numerous advantages for this kind of approach. It is constructed around two major poles: the mother, who is hanging the laundry to dry and watching her son, and the boy, Ahmad, who tries to do his homework and realizes that he must bring the book back to his friend at all costs. A third, secondary pole is the baby who is only present as a permanent "demand" for care, a disruptive "excessive" element in the dual mother-son relationship. Every child can identify with this situation (having experienced a similar one himself), where a peer is caught between his parent's interdiction and the urgent necessity of transgressing this law. You can recount the scene and its principal narrative stakes (its scenic "plan") and make clear, with a floor-plan or a simple model, the space of the courtyard. Students can then be invited to imagine how they would approach the scene and thereby think through principles of filming, the primary axes and points of view, and even a modest introduction to decoupage.

This exercise can take on multiple variations. For example, you can perform it before showing the film, but just after having recounted the story in broad strokes and situated the chosen scene and its stakes in the story. The students will thus have no prior idea of the film's style.

43 Antoine de Baecque and Jacques Parsi, *Conversations avec Manoel de Oliveira*, ed. Cahiers du cinéma, 1996.

You can also make the opposite choice to initially show only the portion of film that precedes the scene: the students will thus have incorporated, intuitively, certain major aspects of the film's style (the mostly fixed camera, for example, the long takes, the rarity of reverse-shots) and will undoubtedly have been influenced by them, even if only unconsciously – but the same is true for the director, who knows that after several days of shooting, the realm of possibility has already been limited to the extent that the choices already made will influence the choices left to make. "The style of a film," Manoel de Oliveira wrote, "is not really defined until after having filmed the first dozen shots. We then become prisoners, in a way."[43] Pasolini, similarly convinced that the first days of filming lay the foundations for the film's style by constraining the range of possibilities, tells how he realized, at the end of a week of shooting, over the course of an anguished night, that he had been wrong about certain stylistic choices from the start, and that he was headed for aesthetic disaster if he persisted in filming *The Gospel According to Matthew* as he had begun it – that is, by re-sanctifying with his camera the already-sacred.

FRAGMENT AND WHOLE

In the act of cinematic creation, one of the greatest difficulties, and the cause of many failures, resides in the fact that, in spite of the appearance of collective labor, a single person holds an idea of the film in its future entirety in his mind, even if it is always vague and poorly defined in parts. The fact that shooting a film requires a team effort makes no difference: at the center of cinematic creation there is always an individual.

Frank Capra, though he worked in the Hollywood studio system, where an army of technicians and specialized crews offloaded a great many decisions and responsibilities from the director, wrote in his autobiography: "All directors ... have this common problem: keeping each day's work in correct relationship to the story as a whole. Scenes shot out of time and context must fit into their exact spot in the mosaic of the finished film, with their exact shadings in mood, suspense, and growing relationships of love or conflict. This is, as one can imagine, the most important and most difficult part of directing, and the main reason why films, perforce, are the director's 'business.'"[44]

The problem, for the filmmaker, consists in making irreversible decisions every day, for every shot, whose merits the film as a whole, which still only exists in his head (for the screenplay is but a meagre skeleton without the flesh), will only validate much later, often months in the future. The painter, too, lays down his brushstrokes one by one, but it is enough for him merely to step back in order to see the effect of one brushstroke on the whole canvas, which he can view in its entirety. The filmmaker lays down his strokes "blindly," and can only guess at their cumulative effect, the resulting rhythm, their harmony or discord.

This question of the whole and the fragment is at the heart of the act of cinematic creation. Eisenstein framed it this way: "the creative process ... proceeds in the following manner. Before the inner vision, before the perception of the creator, hovers a given image, emotionally embodying his theme. The task that confronts him is to transform this image into a few basic *partial representations* which, in their combination and juxtaposition, shall evoke in the consciousness and feelings of the spectator, reader, or auditor, that same initial general image which originally hovered before the creative artist."[45]

The filmmaker has in mind a comprehensive image to which he will give embodiment and reality via the "detailed representations" that shots present. It is easy to see the element of gambling in this operation, which can essentially only function through intuition and "pre-vision." The gamble is that these fragments, placed end to end, will end up reconstituting a (very complex) object where the viewer will rediscover the initial emotion that launched the desire to create, to make a film. Pessoa said it differently, but the idea was the same: in art, "our sensations must be expressed in such a way that they create an object that will become a sensation for others."[46]

And the partial choices that contribute to the creation of this composite object are, by their nature, utterly heterogeneous: a choice of color, of intonation, of a piece of a costume, all

44 Frank Capra, *The Name above the Title*, New York: Random House, 1985, p. 245.

45 S. M. Eisenstein, *The Film Sense* (in *Film Form and The Film Sense*), trans. Jay Leyda, New York: Meridian Books, 1957, p. 30–31.

46 Fernando Pessoa, *Fragments d'un voyage immobile*, Rivages Poche/Petite Bibliothèque n. 42, 1991.

have as much of an effect on the final mental image (which the viewer will accumulate over the course of the film, and will carry with him upon leaving the screening) as the more "linguistic" choices – which are often the only choices that pedagogy concerns itself with – such as dialogue or camera movements. Artistic equilibrium, which gives the film its singularity as a work of art, depends on a thousand factors, impossible to control in a strictly rational way. Jean Renoir spoke of this, as always, with great simplicity and intelligence:

"The most difficult thing is that the artistic equilibrium is different for each person, and personally, I have never been able to convince myself that this equilibrium should be derived solely from the story. I spend my time reestablishing the equilibrium in a film, but the idea of reestablishing it only through elements of the 'plot' doesn't enter my mind. You can reestablish the equilibrium with an object on a table, with a color – if it's a color film – with a line that means nothing but that has more or less weight than the previous one."[47]

Beginning with sequence analysis, students can be made aware of the fact that filmmakers, in the great majority of cases, do not think about the scene as one shot after another, in single file, but generally endeavor to have an idea of the whole that is manifested in the choice of principal camera axis, for example. A filmmaker rarely moves through a scene by deciding on an axis for each shot as he goes along.

47 Jean Renoir, *Renoir on Renoir: Interviews, Essays, and Remarks*, op. cit., p. 93–94.

This would take too much time away from filming, since it would require changing the camera's position, the lights, the placement of the boom, and so on for each shot. But above all, the filmmaker cannot have any control over the way in which the assembly of these shots will affect the viewer later, notably in terms of his identification in the scene. All filmmakers know that depending on the axes selected, with a strictly identical screenplay, the viewer will identify more or less with one or the other character, or with one or another position in the psychic structure that the scene sets up (for example, the role of aggressor or victim). Generally, the filmmaker starts by posing the broad question of the viewer's future perception of the scene: in this scene, do I want a future viewer to identify more, for example, with the aggressor or with the victim? Do I want to primarily provoke suspense (allowing the viewer to see, early in the shot, the character posing a danger to the hero) or surprise (choosing a different axis where the viewer will be as surprised as the hero by the arrival of the aggressor into the field of vision)? It is on the basis of this overall choice that the filmmaker will begin to choose certain principles – two or three fundamental axes, for example. The selection of details, then, shot by shot, will be in part determined by these global principles.

One of the dangers of the storyboard and the overly hasty scene segmentation, in school settings, is that students haphazardly start drawing images one after another, without having been asked to think a bit, first, about the whole of the scene, and about its effects on a future viewer, before leaping into the shot-by-shot. If a student has lined up twelve vignettes, as in a comic strip, and thus believes himself to have visualized the scene, that doesn't mean he has *thought through* the segmentation. If we are content to teach students to think "in detail," without posing the crucial question of the perilous, difficult relationship – at once very abstract and very concrete – between the whole and the detail in cinema, there is every chance that we will distort the reality of the act of cinematic creation. A well-thought-out pedagogy of the fragment entails a pedagogy of the relation of the fragment to the whole. But thinking through this relationship should not be limited to analyzing the editing as a *series of shots* (pieces spliced together): it is essential, in order to avoid distorting your subject, to think of it as a mental operation, where the series of shots is not the first question that presents itself to the creator. In the mental vision that the filmmaker has of his film before making it, there is not yet a series, but only a kind of multi-faceted image. Nabokov, yet again, wrote of the novelist at work: "Time and sequence cannot exist in the author's mind because no time element and no space element had ruled the initial vision. If the mind were constructed on optional lines and if a book could be read in the same way as a painting is taken in by the eye, that is without the bother of working from left to right and without the absurdity of beginnings and ends, this would be the ideal way of appreciating a novel, for thus the author saw it at the moment of its conception."[48]

Robert Bresson is undoubtedly one of the filmmakers who formulated with the greatest acuity this idea of cinema as fragmentation that reconstructs an initial comprehensive image that belongs only to the filmmaker, a mental image that he cannot "show" to anyone: "Many people are needed in order to make a film, but only one who makes, unmakes, remakes his images and sounds, returning at every second to the initial impression or sensation which brought these to birth and is incomprehensible to the other people."[49]

MAKING DECISIONS

There is a temporality of creation that is particular to cinema, determined by an economy that dictates the conditions of decision-making, at the very heart of the act of creation. Analysis has at its disposal a free-floating temporality in relation to a finished, stable object. As soon as the film exists, and a person has access to it, he can spend an afternoon analyzing a shot from *Une partie de campagne* – indeed, he can spend years analyzing an entire film – if he has made it the object of his university studies. It is the legitimate privilege of the analyst (or, quite simply, of the connoisseur) to take all the time that he deems appropriate to get to know a film. The important thing is to avoid flattening the results of this analysis – all of the logical and aesthetic coherences that it brings to light – with whatever presided over Jean

48 Vladimir Nabokov, *Lectures on Literature*, op. cit., p. 379–380.
49 Robert Bresson, *Notes on Cinematography*, op. cit., p. 61.

Renoir's decision-making, stuck on set due to rain, with a deadline determined by the start of the next film's shoot, which would have already been scheduled, and for the sake of which he would end up abandoning the first. There is also, here, an absolutely fundamental difference between cinema and other art forms. The writer – unless he is the author of bestsellers, and has promised to submit his manuscript to his editor on a date that is approaching too quickly – is faced with a relatively flexible timeframe, which he manages according to his own rhythm, or at least with a certain amount of room to maneuver. When it comes to decisions, he can put them off until a later date, take time to mull them over: he is entitled to make corrections and have second thoughts. He can say to himself: "today I am in no condition to write, or I don't want to, I'll write tomorrow," or even: "I'll skip over this part that's 'going badly,' I'll come back to it in a week." And even after having finished, he can still decide to throw his manuscript in the wastebasket and rewrite it. He has before him a much more elastic temporality than the filmmaker.

In the ordinary social conditions surrounding creative practice in cinema, this is almost never the case, with just a few exceptions among filmmakers – Chaplin or Godard, for example – who were given the means (in terms of their relationship to the production process) to manage their time on set differently, to not shoot on days when inspiration was lacking, to start over on a scene that didn't please them in rushes, to bend the shooting time to their own personal creative rhythms. Chaplin could shoot the same film over two or three years, because he was in charge of the means of production, and he alone was left to decide whether the film was definitively finished, and could be shown to the public. If, at any point, he was struggling with a scene, he could stop filming for two or three months, in order to figure out what wasn't working and fix it. If he realized, after several weeks of shooting, that he had made a casting error, he would throw out all of the exposed film and start over from the beginning with a new actress. Godard, for certain films, was also able to shoot for several months, at his own rhythm rather than one dictated by a production's external schedule, a bit like a writer. But such conditions remain quite exceptional in cinema, where the majority of filmmakers are obliged to play the game according to the rules of industrial production, and at times to find their groove within those rules, including with regard to a shooting timeline, where the obligation to finish can sometimes be a useful one, like any other constraint. Amateur filmmakers, and those described as experimental, have always enjoyed the freedom to film at their own pace and according to their own wishes. Jonas Mekas spent years filming footage of his own life precisely because he did not have time to make the films that he wanted to make, in order to "keep his hand in the game," as it were, while waiting for the opportunity to shoot a "real" film – until, that is, the day when he realized that this quasi-commonplace footage *actually constituted his work*, a work of art that would deserve to be more fully present in cinema studies courses as an example of sovereign freedom from any code, and as a model of a cinema of total sensation captured in a collection of partial mini-perceptions.

The majority of filmmakers must adhere to a work plan, devised according to a strictly limited timeframe (time, in cinema, is often worth a great deal of money), that requires them, say, to shoot a delicate love scene next Wednesday morning at nine o'clock, because that's the day when all of the production elements needed for the scene will be present: the sets, the actors, and so on. And on that day, at nine in the morning, the filmmaker will need to film his love scene no matter what happens, even though it is supposed to take place at night, even if he's not inspired, even if the actor has a cold and the actress arrives on set with a zit on her lip. These are the glorious constraints of cinema, and often of students in the classroom, where time is also the most precious commodity, especially in middle and high school. Students sometimes have a single afternoon to shoot their film, because that's the only time they've managed to wrest away from the already tightly scheduled timetable of the classroom. For once, then, the situation in a school setting is not so different from the conditions of filmmaking. Still, it's necessary to ensure that students are somewhat prepared for those conditions in advance, and that the constraints do not trigger defensive strategies (an excessively rigid preparation, for example) that would backfire on the only end result that matters: to provide an experience of creation.

In 99% of cases, in cinema, decisions are made within very strict time constraints, and under a great deal of pressure, all while being more or less irreclaimable. It is imperatively important to take this crucial question of speed into account. When you watch a film, you have the impression that all of the choices were made with a certain amount of conscientiousness and judiciousness. In fact, a significant portion of the decisions that will constitute the reality of a film are made very quickly, with a hastiness that does not always – or often – allow for the decision maker to rationally consider all of the terms of every choice. Art is often a matter of haphazardly, and intuitively, resolving questions that have not necessarily been asked. The painter's brushstroke obeys, in part, a logical decision (this blue will play off of the yellow in the restricted palette that the painter has assigned himself for this canvas), but it's the body, the rhythm of the arm and the hand, the artist's intuition that will inscribe in this manner – unique and rationally inexplicable – this stroke of blue paint at this spot on the canvas. The act of decision-making in cinema is always a mix of rationality, of intention, *and* of intuition, instinct, reflex – except when what's produced is not art but pure commercialized media.

The young Godard's famous formulation remains quite beautiful and very valuable: "Cinema is permanence by chance." The "chance" is everything in a shot, even the most concrete elements, that is out of the filmmaker's control and that occurs only once, at the precise moment of a given take: this animal or that passerby entering the camera's field of view, the shape of this cloud at the moment that the camera was filming, that fleeting uncontrollable intonation uttered by the actor. Cinema is also, at certain moments, a "reflexive" activity. To be a good filmmaker is to have good reflexes, to make the right decision at the right moment, which sometimes passes in a fraction of a second, even if you don't know exactly why you're making that choice. Luck, even more in cinema than elsewhere, is bald at the back of the head, and fleeting: if you do not catch it by the hair at the precise moment that it looks you in the face, it will be too late to seize it two seconds later, when it will have turned on its heels. Classical analysis concludes, obtusely, that choices involve conceptualization, and time. Often in cinema there are choices that must be made – multiple, simultaneous, tangled choices – without really having time for making decisions.

There is, however, one phase in the act of cinematic creation where this question of speed is presented in a less constraining manner. The phase I'm referring to is editing, during which the filmmaker is in a much better position to think through and rationalize his choices, to call them into question, to make them and remake them, to grope in the dark. And it's increasingly true with digital editing, which allows the filmmaker, in his own home, to familiarize himself with the rushes, to try different edits, different takes, different drafts of his scenes, at his leisure, at any hour of the day or night. In classical montage, the filmmaker

who wanted to try a new "version" of a scene was obligated to "break apart" the earlier version, to make the decision to undo the existing montage in order to construct a new one using the same film, which he would need to re-cut and rejoin differently. Today, where we can easily hoard all of the attempted montages, all of the variations, the definitive moment of decision can be long postponed, perpetually put off until tomorrow, until the obligation to "deliver" a product to a producer or a distributor forces a decision. And still, the filmmaker always potentially has the option of someday remaking the film in a new version, shorter or longer, for the DVD release, for example. The day is not far off where the "theatrical" version of a film will be considered by the filmmaker to be a sort of compromise with the commercial demands of distribution and exhibition, while awaiting the "director's cut" that will be released a bit later on DVD: the process has already begun.

THE PLAN, THE REALITY, THE ACTOR

In Godard's *Hail Mary*, an actress delivers this very beautiful line: "We are amazed that an image arrives, where there could have been nothing." In creative analysis, you might say instead: "We are amazed that an image is what it is, where it could have been any other." With every shot or scene, one must think back to the moment where there was only a narrative and aesthetic "plan" for this scene, and a multitude of choices still to be made, choices of all kinds: sets, costumes, movements, lighting, rhythms, an actor's gestures or intonations. The shot that one sees is always a hybrid of the "plan" for the scene, existing prior to the actual staging of the scene; certain general principles to be applied to the whole film, determined at the start; and the decisions made shot by shot, scene by scene. These decisions belong simultaneously to an element of instinct that resembles the impetus behind a painter's brushstroke, and to an encounter with the real.

There always exists – though it might remain indistinct, unwritten and unspoken – a "plan" for the scene inside the head of the filmmaker preparing to film. It might reside in a classical screenplay, a dialogue scribbled at the last moment on a scrap of paper, a handful of sketches or a floor-plan, or just a few words said aloud; but no one can film without a plan, even in the short term. Every filmmaker, then, depending on his temperament, the kind of film he wants to make, and the economic conditions under which he works, will find what he deems to be the most reasonable relationship between this "plan" and its actualization. This relationship can be one of simple execution: the process of filming, and then of editing, become the most faithful possible translation of the plan. This describes the rather panoramic cinema of "closed storyboards," which gave rise to the greatest films of Hitchcock, Fritz Lang, and Kubrick, but can also lead to films that are utterly stifled by excessive control, where life can no longer get room to breathe. The relationship can be one of semi-improvisation: the film is inscribed on a canvas where the scenes are already sketched in, but the dialogue is written day by day, depending

on what the film shoot offers in the way of atmosphere, where suggestions come equally often from the scenery, the actors, and the weather. This is the method used in a majority of Rivette's films and certain films by Rohmer, including *The Green Ray*, as well as in Wenders's early works. In France, it owes a great deal to the pioneering films of Jean Rouch. And long before the Nouvelle Vague – which advocated in its early years for a more "open" screenplay than what was then typical in French studio films – it was the preferred method of the masters Rossellini and Renoir.

The act of cinematic creation is often situated between these two extremes, especially in classroom settings where the obsessive focus on control is unrealistic and deceptive given the precariousness of available time and resources: absolute control of the Hitchcockian variety is the most expensive kind of filmmaking, for reality does not give up its hold so easily when one lacks the means and the manpower to reconstruct it in the studio.

Unlike the writer or the composer, the filmmaker (whether he shoots his films in the studio or in natural settings, whether he makes documentaries or fiction films) deals with reality, with objects in the real world without which he would have nothing to film, at least until very recently, when entirely digital images have begun to open new possibilities of image-making that can produce an effect of realism without any encounter with the real. It's a safe bet, however, that the kind of cinema where a camera records something in front of it – whether staged or unvarnished reality – still has a bright future ahead. This kind of cinema addresses a need for the viewer that the digital will never be able to eliminate: the need to see real bodies, real landscapes, faces on which a viewer can follow the changes imprinted by the passage of time from film to film. Cinema entails watching actors age who fall in one's own age group; a long take of a face in close-up is "seeing death at work," according to Jean Cocteau's formulation. For André Bazin, this mechanical act of capturing a unit of space-time, of a reality – staged or not staged – constitutes the ontological vocation of cinema as a specific art, since, after all, the act of telling a story is the legacy of novelistic and theatrical literature. It was in the name of cinema's ontological vocation that Godard could claim that "in cinema, the story must be seen, not told." The particularity of cinema is that this reality, whatever it is, will always resist, in one way or another, the "plan" for a shot, a scene, a storyline, and that a good filmmaker, once again, is the one who takes this resistance into account, who leans into it and turns it to his artistic advantage for the sake of his film. This resistant reality is, first, the space that existed before any mise-en-scène, it's the set dressings, whether natural or not (a door in the studio is as real an object as a door in a natural setting), it's the weather (the history of cinema is full of masterpieces filmed in meteorological conditions that were disastrous compared with the projections of the screenplay and the production plan, from *L'Atalante* to *Rules of the Game*), it's above all, always, the actors.

Indeed, the actor – even if he is who the filmmaker wanted, even if the screenplay was written with him already in mind, even if he "gets along well" with the director – is always the most resistant element, the most surprising, indeed the most dispossessing for the filmmaker, relative to the film as he imagined it mentally while writing the screenplay. This is because of the fact that the actor, all at once, on the set, incarnates – with his body, with his own particular movements and rhythms, his intonations, his scansion of words in the dialogue – a character who, prior to that moment, was nothing but a character on paper, and all of this is experienced by the director as a kind of dispossession of the encompassing mental image, with its vague contours, that he had held previously. The actor is the most resistant element in cinema, especially when the filmmaker realizes that this embodiment strays (as is almost always the case) from the mental image of the scene that he had built up, or even simply from the way he had imagined a line would be spoken. A dialogue that one hears, while writing it, with his inner ear is never the same as the dialogue that comes out of the mouth of the actor, who necessarily brings to it the grain of his voice, an interpretive coloring, his own rhythm.

The good filmmaker is one who constructs something new – something which is not entirely what he had "pre-viewed" – *with* the unique contributions of the actor who puts up resistance. He reassesses, from shot to shot, intuitively, with his eyes and ears, the parts that he will need to correct (in order to move in the direction of his initial idea) and the parts that he will need to accept, in the actor's perform-ance, as an acceptable (or even beneficial) transformation of the director's imagined ver-sion of the character and the film. This process undoubtedly demonstrates the most lively, and most difficult to control, aspect of cinematic di-rection. Everything else – lighting, framing, cutting – can be learned and more or less con-trolled, unlike this living relationship with the actor, which must be reestablished each day, for each shot. This explains the failure of many early short films, including those made in the most prestigious film schools, where all of the energy in a film shoot is mobilized to impecca-bly control all of the technical parameters, while the poor actors, left to themselves, neg-lected by the director – whose primary concern is to prove his capacity for control – are thrown at the last second into a shot, where they are necessarily disoriented and often bad, none of which is their fault in the least. The actor is an essential component of the film that the viewer experiences: if he is poorly cast or untalented, the best of screenplays will come to nothing, and no technical or linguistic mastery will be able to do anything about it. It is therefore in-dispensable, in any treatment of films in the classroom, to teach children to observe actors and their acting, in the films being studied, with the same attention that one gives to the frame or the camera movements. Primary schools take this kind of approach very rarely, as though it were pointless. But observing and describing the way in which an actor performs a scene (and the way in which the filmmaker

articulates his mise-en-scène through this ques-tion of the actor) is one of the richest and most concrete points of entry to get at the very heart of fiction cinema. Luc Moullet's book *Politique des acteurs* suggests invaluable, and utterly easy to use, avenues into this analysis of the role and performance of the actor.[50]

Anyone who, in an educational context, would refuse to take this encounter with reality into account as an essential element of the cinematic act of creation, in the name of tightening one's grip on the idea of control, would be gravely distorting the very nature of the cinema that he meant to pass down. Giving students the means to achieve a certain mastery in the ap-proach to films is one of the objectives of the educator, but the greatest pedagogical danger would be to reduce cinema appreciation to the elements that derive from control. In doing so, one would inescapably fail to appreciate cin-ema as a perceptive and sensitive art form, and as the "written language of reality."

NEGATIVITY AND THE ILLOGICAL

Yves Caumont, a filmmaker who often gives talks in pedagogical settings, has developed an "exercise" for introducing students to the cre-ative act, in which he compares, one after an-other, three different cinematic versions of the same scene in *Madame Bovary* – the scene where she receives the letter of rejection from Rodolphe in a basket of apricots and, violently

50 Luc Moullet, *Politique des acteurs*, ed. Cahiers du cinéma, 1993.

upset, nearly falls from the window of the attic where she has hidden from her husband in order to read the letter. The narrative "out-line" for the scene is roughly the same for Jean Renoir, Claude Chabrol, and (to a lesser ex-tent) Vincente Minnelli: to show the distress and disorientation that seizes this woman upon reading this letter of farewell, while her hus-band is there, in the house, an unwanted spec-tator to her turmoil and her distress. The expe-rience of this comparison is utterly illuminat-ing: the same "content" and the same narrative situations absolutely do not produce the same choices on the part of three different filmmak-ers. Renoir and Chabrol both include *the* shot, seen from outside the house, where Emma is at the edge of the attic window, framed by it. Chabrol includes an extreme low-angle shot where the camera, on the floor, seems to pull the woman toward the drop. Renoir chooses an opposite angle: he places his camera above the window and films Emma's vertigo with a "high-angle shot."

The question here is not, of course, the eter-nal question of adaptation, but rather of cre-ative choice. In this dramatic situation, where a woman teeters on the edge of the abyss in a moment of great distress – which one finds in numerous films that bear no relation to Flaubert's novel, notably in the films of Hitch-cock, who liked very much to suspend his ac-tresses on the edge of the void, on riverbanks or steep cliffs – deciding on the sightline from which the camera will "attack" the character is a crucial choice. Let's imagine a class, with no knowledge of Renoir's version, analyzing

Chabrol's shot according to the classical schol-arly logic of analysis. There's a good chance that it could easily be demonstrated that Chabrol, as a good filmmaker, had chosen THE right solution using logical reasoning. This would lead to something like the follow-ing: "the filmmaker chose the low-angle shot because that's the best angle from which to see the actress's body teetering and to make us tremble with the (delicious) fear of seeing her fall and crash onto the ground beside us, right in front of our eyes." Let's now imagine the conclusions that would be drawn by another class, analyzing only Renoir's film with no knowledge of Chabrol's: "the great filmmaker (who *a priori* always makes the right choice, since he is a great filmmaker) chose the high angle in order to make us see the appeal of the abyss beneath the heroine, so as to better allow us to share her elevated point of view and her vertigo." What can be said of these two analy-ses? Each is as convincing as the other, and both prove only one thing: that any short-circuiting, deterministic demonstration (the filmmaker made this choice to produce that effect) is reas-suring (every choice is justifiable, with a greater or lesser number of analytical contortions de-pending on the case, in the voluntaristic logic of the celebrated and formidable "meaning" of the director) but doesn't quite align with the reality (a thousand times less rational) of the act of creation. To return to that famous shot of the woman at the edge of the abyss (or be-lieving herself to be), it is likely that the choice of camera angle depended first on an overall conception of the scene and the setting that the filmmaker wanted to build for his viewer, and that Chabrol's solution (to be in the position of a person on the ground, awaiting the woman's fall) and Renoir's solution (to share a point of view that is closer to that of the woman herself) are relatively opposed. But I do not doubt, for my part, that at the last second, both men could have made the opposite choice.

What is obvious, in comparing Renoir's version with Chabrol's, is that there is a great deal more "chaos" in Renoir's, where the logic of simply "communicating" the meaning of the scene is more than once disrupted, attacked from the rear, even contradicted. We find in Renoir's version many inexplicable elements, notably in the strange framings, which resist any simplistic logic, including the logic that we surmise to be the logic of the scene for Renoir himself. Art (even as socialized and industrial an art as cinema can be) is that which resists pure logic, and which clings to the intuition and sovereignty of the artist; it is where the artist enacts choices, makes decisions through which he imprints his underlying personality, his obsessions, his aversions and his tastes, and all of what comprises his unique subjectivity. If cinematic creativity only obeyed deductive logic, there would really be only one way to film the shot of Emma on the brink of falling, and all filmmakers with the slightest bit of talent and rationality would adopt the same solution. If schools want to teach cinema as an art, they must discard once and for all the old scholastic idea according to which there is one, and only one, right way to say something, and one right way to film a scene or a shot in cinema.

If there is really art in cinema, it is what's at work in the "personal art coefficient" that Marcel Duchamp – who knew what he was talking about in matters of artistic creation – wrote about with great clarity: "In the creative act, the artist goes from intention to realization through a chain of totally subjective reactions. His struggle toward the realization is a series of efforts, pains, satisfactions, refusals, decisions, which also cannot and must not be conscious, at least on the esthetic plane.

The result of this struggle is a difference between the intention and its realization, a difference which the artist is not aware of.

Consequently, in the chain of reactions accompanying the creative act, a link is missing. This gap which represents the inability of the artist to express fully his intention; this difference between what he intended to realize and did realize, is the personal 'art coefficient' contained in the work.

In other words, the personal 'art coefficient' is like an arithmetical relation between the unexpressed but intended and the unintentionally expressed."[51]

In this formulation, Duchamp postulates that every creator has a plan, an intention, a direction, an "outline," inevitably transformed by the work being carried out. For Duchamp it is not a matter of claiming that anything is possible in the name of an unlimited artistic liberty that obviously does not make much

51 Marcel Duchamp, "The Creative Act," in *Salt Seller: The Writings of Marcel Duchamp*, ed. Michel Sanouillet and Elmer Peterson, New York: Oxford University Press, 1973, p. 139.

sense, and which can be of no help to someone trying to learn about art. But he takes into account the fact that the accomplishment of his initial plan partly eludes him, for the precise reasons that make him an artist and not a mere translator or subordinate to his own plan. Robert Bresson instructed himself to "not have the soul of an executant (of my own projects)" and to "find, for each shot, a new pungency over and above what I had imagined. Invention (re-invention) on the spot."[52] It would be quite damaging to teach our students – following a strong pedagogical tendency – to become their own subordinates, too submissive to their own written or sketched-out plan. An educator must find the right attitude between taking a plan into account and respecting Duchamp's "art coefficient": what was planned but not actualized in a film, and what was expressed but not planned.

"There is no painting," wrote Samuel Beckett. "There are only paintings. … All you can say about them is that they translate, with a greater or lesser degree of loss, absurd and mysterious jabs at the image, and that they are more or less adequate at capturing obscure internal tensions. As for determining for yourself the degree of adequacy, such is out of the question, since you are not in the skin of he who experiences the tensions. Indeed, he himself has no knowledge of it most of the time. … Losses and profits are of equal value in the economy

of art, where the second-person pronoun illuminates what is said, and where all presence is absence. All you will ever know about a painting is how much you love it (and, at most, why you love it, if that interests you)."[53]

There is often, in the creative act, a negative force that is part of the drive to create. One film that renders this force especially visible is Clouzot's *Le Mystére Picasso*, an invaluable film for understanding the non-logical aspects of the act of creation, or in any case those aspects which obey a different logic. In the film we see paintings in the course of being made, which offer us precious access to something that is never seen: all of the paintings that are *underneath* the finished, signed painting, and that engendered it. We get a glimpse, if you will, of how the painting hanging on the wall of the museum was never anything, for Picasso, but the cessation of possibilities. He starts by painting the head of a bull, and it becomes a beach, or vice-versa. One sometimes has the impression, upon looking at a painting in the process of being painted, that Picasso, at some point, reaches a kind of equilibrium, where the canvas appears to us to be perfectly "in place," finished, but Picasso rarely stops at this seeming equilibrium; he sets about hammering away at it, painting over it, ruining it (in our eyes, of course), "breaking" it open, finally stopping at a point that seems to us to be more contingent, unstable, "warped," than certain earlier points had been. There is sometimes almost a kind of fury in him to blacken or strike out whole sections of a painting that had seemed to us –

52 Robert Bresson, *Notes on Cinematography*, op. cit., p. 1.
53 Samuel Beckett, *Le monde et le pantalon*, éditions de Minuit, 1990.

mere spectators of the act of creation – to be harmonious, stable, finished.

In cinema, Godard's work is entirely exemplary of this negative impulse at work in the act of creation. I am thinking, for example, about the scene of the factory workers' union meeting in *Passion*. Like all filmmakers, Godard begins by organizing the scene to make it intelligible, arranging its elements in order to film them in the manner laid out in the screenplay, for this scene has a role to play in the overall story of the film: it shows Isabelle Huppert's role in the strike that is being planned, and her relationships with the other workers. But suddenly, at the moment of filming, Godard notices an extra in the background, with a ray of sunlight striking her red hair, and he places his camera not at the logical position from which it would have taken in the meaning of the scene and endowed it with maximum legibility, but behind this extra. He is no longer in "the right place" with regard to the immediate intelligibility of the scene, but he has happened upon a real, new desire to film this shot – a desire that owes nothing to the screenplay. Godard, in this case, never sacrifices his desire for the shot to the need for clarity of communication. Bresson quotes Auguste Renoir: "You must paint the bouquet from the side which you did not arrange." If the filmmaker arranges his bouquet and then positions his camera in the right place – the place of greatest legibility

– he risks not having any surprise, any life, any untidiness, any fresh sensations. He must arrange the bouquet, but sometimes, he must dare, at the last second, to film from a different angle. This illogical, impulsive element, which can seem to be detrimental, and to undermine the scene, is an integral part of the act of creation, if it is to avoid being too sterilized and subservient to the laws of pure consumption.

Primary education has always feared the void and the negative. It is true that it is the mission of education to teach how to construct, before talking about forces that counteract this act of construction, and which are often a part of the creative impulse. I am not certain, however, that the resulting defensive analyses – where everything, in the scene or film being analyzed, obeys a beautiful logic of construction, of which the analyst constructs a flawless and too-convincing model – do not sometimes betray the very objects they are trying to grasp. Can one seriously analyze a film by Jean Renoir without taking into account the maxim of his father Auguste about the unarranged side of the bouquet? And when it comes to introducing students to the creative process, does one really have the right to conceal the negative elements that sometimes constitute the living force of tension without which the act of creation risks having no spark of life, but only rhetorical academicism and enslavement to mere communication?

VIII

Creating in the Classroom:
Stepping into Creative Practice

CREATION IS NOT THE OPPOSITE OF ANALYSIS

The major pedagogical illusion, in matters of creativity, involves acting as though the act of creation obeys (like a mirror image) the same deductive logic as analysis. In this view, it would be enough to borrow the logic that analysis applies to a finished film or scene, and apply it "in reverse" at the moment of creation. If one has been taught, to cite a persistent stereotypical example, that Orson Welles filmed a particular shot in *Citizen Kane* from a low angle "in order to" aggrandize a character, and that he filmed some other character, in *A Touch of Evil*, from a high angle "in order to" belittle him, then it would suffice to ask oneself the corresponding question – "do I want to aggrandize or belittle this character?" – in order to choose one's own angle of attack on some poor actor, who would wonder why his director was behaving towards him like a little Orson Welles, with whom his director shared neither the charisma nor the corpulence.

These kinds of short-circuits are often, for the teacher, a way of reassuring himself with regard to his competence and expertise as a teacher in a field that he doesn't necessarily feel he has mastered. There is, of course, an element of conscious logic in the many simultaneous choices that the filmmaker must make at

every instant, and which he is able to credibly justify to his director of photography or his performers ("I prefer to use this camera angle because it allows me to see this character enter before the protagonist"). But there are equally decisive choices that are made intuitively, with the private conviction that they are the right choices, even if the filmmaker is unable or unwilling to justify them to a skeptical crew. It is often the case that the director "invents" a logical justification, after the fact, for this or that choice, for which the real reasons are very difficult to communicate to a third party.

Added to this difficulty is the fact that, given the number of decisions that must be made for a single shot, the idealized vision of a filmmaker resolving those decisions, one after another, according to a sort of imaginary *checklist*, before beginning to shoot, is absurd. These decisions are all different in form and function, and are not merely linguistic: the filmmaker is equally called upon to decide the color of a blouse, the movement of an actor, and the type of lighting needed for this shot and for that take. They are as strongly determined by taste, fear, and rhythm, as they are by (linguistic) meaning itself, which educators always have a tendency to overvalue.

We find, in cinema as in the other arts, great critics and theorists who have never had the smallest amount of experience practicing the art in which they specialize. I am convinced, however, that in any instruction in a creative practice, it is best to have a direct and personal experience, however modest, of the practice itself. The difference between *teaching*, in the classical sense, and *instructing*, is a matter of what is required. There will always be something lacking in the instructor who has never had an intimate experience with the creative process and with *what it requires of the practitioner*. For it is really the experience of an exchange, practitioner to practitioner, that's at play in the passing-down of a creative practice, for which it is nearly indispensable to have taken the risk, at least once in one's life, of choosing a position, a camera angle, a distance, a framing, of deciding what must be said, or left unsaid, to the actor, of deciding on his movements, of judging the success of the performance, the speed of the camera's movements, and so on. This experience will necessarily provide the instructor with greater patience and tolerance.

WHY AND FOR WHOM ARE WE FILMING?

It is precisely so that the students can have this experience for themselves that practical creative instruction is indispensable. There is something irreplaceable in this experience, which is enacted as much in the body as in the brain – a knowledge of a different order, which can't be acquired through the mere analysis of films, no matter how well-guided. One does not learn to ski by watching competitive skiing on television, without ever having felt in one's body, with one's muscles, the sensations of different snow conditions, of bumps in the slope, of the speed, the fear, and the joy of skiing.

The experience of creation, which is essential and indispensable, is often in competition with another aim, one which is more visible and easier to evaluate: the goal of producing a group project that can be shown to others, to students' parents, or at specialized festivals. The question arises regularly, with dreadful uniformity, in school settings: for what, and for whom, are we filming? Must we share the result? With whom? Under what conditions?

In cinema, it is rare that anyone makes a film just for himself, unless it is in the mode of a private journal. Today, thanks to small "pocket-sized" digital cameras, many people – considerably more than in the age of Super 8, or even in the days of bulkier camcorders – film primarily for themselves (initially, at least), much in the way that one might keep a journal or take photos. With this new kind of first-person cinematic practice, no one would feel obligated to finish a film, or to show it to anyone, or even to develop it from the raw-footage stage into a concrete film-object. The "boom" in autobiographical cinema over the last few years undoubtedly has something to do with this transformation, which has allowed films like those of Jonas Mekas, to take a gratifying example, to escape from the ghetto of "experimental cinema" to which they have been confined for over thirty years. It is an evolution that creative arts education must take into account: today it's possible to imagine free exercises in first-person filmmaking, and we have at our disposal tools that would make them practical. There can be no doubt that these solitary exercises will change the game with regard to the decisive moment of "the first time."

Nevertheless, producing a finished, audience-worthy film-object is still the objective of every filmmaker who participates in any system of production, however modest. Primary schools, if they want to be spaces of exchange and socialization, are obliged to take into account this goal of "showing off what we made."

Once this principle has been set down, all of the dangers come into play. The main danger is that educators will make this kind of exhibition the whole point of any creative exercise in the classroom, and will thus lead it astray from its deeper purpose. In school settings, the primary goal of making a film is not the finished film-object itself, as a "product," but the irreplaceable experience of a creative process, even a very modest one. There is, in the act of creating, a virtue of understanding that cannot be gained except through the act itself. The "success" of the film-object, inasmuch as it is able to charm an audience of students' parents, or even of their peers, does not in any way prove that "the exercise was profitable," to borrow the aforementioned line from *Moonfleet*. I often have the opposite suspicion, watching these films be embraced by an enthusiastic audience, that it is precisely these parental viewers who have been the least effective teachers to the children who made the films, being too invested in a concern for communication, a desire for efficiency, and thus an obedience to the most "ironclad" rules.

The tradition of the "end-of-the-year show" is very important in French educational culture, with its blend of inanity and blissful self-satisfaction. The ultimate nightmare would be to make films, in the classroom, geared toward their future success on the clap-o-meter at the performance at the end of the year, for parents or any other audience. It is the mission of the adults who guided these productions to make use of these screenings in order to educate, in some small way, the parents in the audience, showing them the films for what they are – as traces of an experience, as steps in a creative process – and insisting, above all, on their instructive value. Among the possible solutions, there is the option of showing, as part of the same event, the process (the exercises that preceded the act of making the film, some raw footage, a few different edits of a single scene) and the result of this process. What's more, parents would be more inclined to see these films as something more than a televised spectacle if they had themselves taken part in certain moments of shooting the films, in the background, like an extra support crew (as stage managers or at the sound board, for example), or simply as participants along for the ride.

Making a film that is well-received, and that the audience (even the rigged audience of this kind of performance) "understands," is certainly very gratifying for everyone. The feeling of failure is always painful. And when an audience of one's peers (students from another classroom, for example, since parents are always ready to "admire" whatever their offspring have made) indicates that they "didn't understand the story," the student-directors experience it as a real failure. All of this, however, deserves to be put into perspective and clarified.

Most often, it is because of clumsiness, and a lack of mastery over the cinematic medium and storytelling methods, that the film – clearly envisioned in the minds of those who made it, who were convinced that it would be entirely legible – becomes impenetrable for those receiving it. But after all, no educator would ask a ten-year-old child to draw like Ingres or like a graphic designer. The drawing abilities that you would expect this child to possess (and which would determine one's estimation of the success of his drawing) are not the same as those you would expect to find in a student at the Beaux-Arts – neither technically nor aesthetically, nor even in terms of "exhibition-worthiness." Why would things be any different for cinema? Why would a child, or a group of children, be expected to perfectly master what we know to be the result of a long process of maturation, and not only technically, but with respect to one's general comprehension of the world and of modes of representation? The teacher, or the lecturer, must accept the idea that it is normal for young (or very young) people to work with perspectives and ellipses that are not present in films or television programs made by adult professionals, and that telling a story with sounds and images – simultaneously managing the editing and the mise-en-scène, rhythms and meanings – involves an extraordinary degree of complexity that normally requires years of practice to master. Evaluating the success of a film made by students in Year 4, or even in Year 11, should not (except by sleight-of-hand) follow the same criteria that would be used to evaluate the success of a short film made by an adult professional. Different factors must be evaluated: the student's engagement in a process, the coherence of the process, the fact that someone really made these choices and put them to the test in the reality of the film shoot or the editing table – in short, the fact that the student had an experience, and that this experience really taught something, by different means than those of teaching in the classical sense of the term.

The danger posed by the fear of failure must not give rise to codified instruction, to submission before the aesthetic or linguistic pseudo-rules that regulate communication. After all, when Godard directed *Eloge de l'amour*, or when Manoel de Oliveira directed *Inquietude*, the viewer had a similarly difficult time "understanding" the screenplay, and still more difficulty with the eventual "message." For these filmmakers – who had previously made films that became clearer with the passage of time – it was not clumsiness that resulted in the opacity or confusion in the films' communication, but rather the high ideas that they both entertained about their art. In any truly creative film there is an element that remains an enigma, that resists, that is never entirely assimilable, legible, at least not at the moment of its appearance. This was true of films that now seem to us as "self-evident" as Jean Renoir's *Rules of the Game*, Dreyer's *Gertrud*, or Jean-Luc Godard's *Contempt*. And perhaps, after all, there is something similar in the resistance that prevents the viewer of *Eloge de l'amour* and the viewer of a film directed by a student in Year 4 from "understanding the story." Godard, too, in a way, worked for so many years on his screenplay, and obsessed so insistently over the film before and after shooting, that he no longer really had the need nor the desire to tell the story, and he ended up only filming crude fragments, without the narrative cohesion or the cause-and-effect succession with which standard productions are obsessed.

In France there are private film schools where they offer accelerated instruction to prepare students to become semi-specialized technicians, more or less competitive on the job market, but where they eliminate any chance that the student might have of someday becoming something of a thinking and feeling "subject" of his own artistic practice. In these schools they mass-produce "television manpower," in the service of received ideas about efficiency. They strictly limit their curricula to teaching codes (without ever interrogating them) that enable students to become efficient technicians: I'm thinking of all the native pseudo-rules of framing, for example, that pave the way for academicism. These kinds of training have more in common with rote machine learning than with a real pedagogy, where it is of the utmost importance that the student be respected as the subjectivity behind the creative act, however modest his role in the film's development.

The work of art is never one hundred percent efficient; it disobeys academic rules, and demands creative intuition and code-defying innovation. As soon as the filmmaker is really present in his work, these codes are always perverted to an extent, distorted, even inverted, and the film necessarily becomes a bit more opaque and resistant. The transparency of the communication should never be the last word, even when it comes to filmmaking in a school setting. If one sets one's sights on the objective of fully domesticating this practice, and thus of making a film that is legible by everyone and accessible to everyone, one necessarily subjugates himself to the most dominant, the "biggest" codes, as does any filmmaker whose goal is total transparency, to make his film perfectly digestible and immediately legible for everyone, without elements of resistance or excess. And one runs the risk of rote proficiency, of efficiency at all costs that casts aside an essential dimension of the artistic impulse: the presence of a singular subjectivity in, and behind, the artwork.

TAKING AWAY THE ACT OF CREATION

This perversion of filmmaking in a school setting, which involves investing everything in, and organizing everything around, the "success" of the final result – an accomplished, appealing, wholly communicative film-object –

often brings about a forfeiture of the creative act. I am not talking about the banal, clumsy forfeiture that happens when an adult makes a film by proxy, on the backs of his students or in their place; such a thing exists, but it is entirely pathological and in the minority, and is not really worth discussing at length. In the case of these adults, without the assistance of a psychoanalyst or a psychologist, there's not much that can be done other than to limit the damage by barring them from this kind of role. I have always simply been wary of the too-emphatic declarations of those who begin by announcing, without ever having been asked, that "the children did everything." Others, more comfortable in their own skin and in their role, thus having a better chance of being good teachers, are more circumspect about what came from the children and what came from a negotiation between the children and the adults, and even what came from the adults themselves. There is no reason, at certain stages in the work of creation, that the adult should not intervene as an adult, as a member of the little community that is executing a project that he, the adult, encouraged. This is a normal productive relationship to be found at the heart of any filmmaking crew. Every director has this conversation with his producer, his technicians, his actors. It's always preferable that the adult occasionally films a shot that has caught his interest, in a manner that is entirely faithful, and accepted, as one of his contributions to the film, rather than performing the manipulation of making a child make the shot that he would have liked to make himself. There has, moreover, always been, in certain arts such as painting, a tradition of direct apprenticeship that entails watching the master at work or painting some small pieces of the canvas that he has entrusted to the apprentices in his studio. This still happens with photography, at the Arles festival, for example, in what's called a "workshop": a "master" of photography takes photos in front of students who watch him work and then try their hand at an identical subject in his wake. It is possible to understand a great deal about art as a result of such an apprenticeship, through observation and direct contagion, and in the simple fact of watching an artist at work. Watching the documentary that a Japanese filmmaker made during the shoot of Abbas Kiarostami's *The Wind Will Carry Us* (under the title *A Week with Kiarostami*),[54] the viewer understands immediately, through direct observation of a filmmaker at work, why his work resembles no other director's today. It is sufficient to see the climate that prevails over the film shoot, the relationships that are forged day after day between the child, the director, and the adult actor and to attend to the slow arrangement of a shot on the bank of the little river, in order to appreciate what gives rise later, onscreen, to the singularity of this film and this filmmaker.

Seeing an artist create does not, of course, reveal the personal key to his creativity, but rather allows the viewer to understand how

54 *A Week with Kiarostami*, directed by Yuji Mohara (Slow Hand Production).

this artist sees, how he approaches his work, how he comports himself relative to creation itself. Watching Matisse paint could never provide the key to the mystery of his creativity, but Matisse's attitude in front of his design, his model, his paint tubes, his palette – this must reveal a great deal about his creative work. Over the course of my *"Cahiers* years," I often went to watch filmmakers work and, contrary to popular belief, I feel that I learned and internalized a great deal as a result of this simple, silent, slantwise observation, even if the essence, the very heart of creation, does not belong to the order of the visible. I had an entirely different critical and analytical approach to Godard's films after seeing him at work – even if what was in his head at the time was utterly opaque and enigmatic – having glimpsed something of the creator that he is, if only in his way of being with the technicians, the actors, the machinery, the temporality of the film shoot.

This is a mode of knowledge transmission that is not used much in primary schools, for it is not communicated through speech and rational constructions. There is, however, something that can be rather directly taught in an experience like, for example, watching someone operate a camera or adjust a frame – on the condition that those watching maintain an attitude of acute observation. This is undoubtedly something to consider revamping in the education system, once art becomes central to teaching. Why shouldn't we sometimes let the professional guest speaker simply do his work, as a craftsman, while we watch him and listen

to him as he simply comments on his actions and his decisions?

The most insidious way of sabotaging students' experience, when implementing creative practice in a school setting, is tied to under- or overestimating the skills and the time that students will have at their disposal. This is what happens every time that a filmmaking project is too ambitious – in terms of length – relative to the real conditions of production. Students might write a fifteen-minute film while only being able to devote two half-days to shooting – wrested with difficulty from the constraining classroom schedule – and four hours to editing, the first of which might be spent resolving problems with transport, digital connections, and wiring. When they realize that they have overestimated their abilities, and especially overestimated what they can actually accomplish in the available timeframe, it will be too late. Each student in the group will have made it a point of honor to finish the film as they had envisioned it, and the crisis will make the experience itself recede into the background. The film to be finished will impose its tyranny over everyone. No one will have any degree of control over anything, and students will no longer have any time at all to reflect on what is happening, in blind obedience to a perfect model of Stakhanovist productivity. In this case, there is no longer any guarantee that anyone will have the slightest experience of a creative process. In terms of creative practice, in school settings, this experience has nothing to do with the fact that a finished film exists, nor that it is celebrated, but rather with the fact that *someone* has made it.

The best filmmakers are those who do not deceive themselves with regard to what kind of film they can make in relation to the real conditions of production that are available to them. Even in a school setting, one must keep in mind the general economics of the little film that one has endeavored to make, for this, too, is part of an education in filmmaking. Instead of dreaming about a film that students will not have time to produce in good conditions, it is more valuable to formulate a work plan as a group, to determine the real amount of time available to students for shooting the film – in an afternoon where, for example, footage must be shot in two different locations, separated by a distance. How much real shooting time at each location will be left, if you subtract the time needed for transportation and set-up? This is the only way to see, in black and white, whether the students have conceived a project that is much too ambitious relative to the real conditions at hand. In cinema, even more than in other arts, the ability to evaluate the time and energy required for a filmmaking project is part of a general understanding of the creative process.

SHORT FILM OR PIECE OF A FEATURE?

The dominant model for filmmaking in schools is naturally the short film, which seems to be virtually the only practical option. The short film should be where students can have the greatest freedom, since it is seemingly a genre with fewer constraints, unlike the stan-dard feature-length film, which must last an hour and a half, tell a story, and be released in theaters. In reality, short films oscillate between freedom and excessive codification. Education generally loves anything that is excessively codified, and which offers easy and convincing methods of decoding. As a result, you might think that the short film would be the perfect format for a school framework, and that its reduced length would facilitate classroom analysis as well as an introduction to creative practice. Things are not that simple, however.

Historically, short student films (intended to be made in the classroom) have long provided an opportunity to dabble in filmmaking, since no one can be sure of their desire to work in cinema until they have experienced it. Such was the case for the Nouvelle Vague filmmakers, who tried their hand at short films in order to seek out their own styles. Their films were often clumsy and cobbled together, but already contained the essence of their idea of cinema. They learned to make films, *their* films, together, in relative freedom, without caring too much, in this formative period, about their audience. The case of *Une histoire d'eau* is paradigmatic: Truffaut jumped at the chance that was offered to him by a flood in the Paris suburbs to film, at great speed, with a camera and a bit of film furnished by the producer Pierre Braunberger, some improvised shots with two actors and a car. Godard then snatched up these rushes, which he himself had not filmed, in order to write sparkling dialogue and narration after the fact, and edit the shots into a lively and inventive montage. This baton-passing between fledgling directors visibly represented a merry and playful apprenticeship.

Today, the short film has too often become a hyper-codified genre, willingly "nouveau riche," practiced by little smart alecks whose primary aim is to produce a calling card capable of seducing a television network. The "calling card" film is the opposite, in my view, of what the student film or the classroom production ought to be. The majority of these formulaic films have a rather unpleasant "show-off" quality about them. The screenplays must be brilliant, the endings climactic, the storylines convoluted, the camera angles bizarre, the lighting conspicuous, the camera movements virtuosic: each shot seems designed to say, above all: "look what I can do." This demonstration is often also useful for showing off the actors' performances, which are willfully excessive, and which underline the element of showing off. In reality this is a way of bypassing the real difficulties of cinema. "What is truly difficult is to make two actors sit face to face, and to make them act out a long dialogue accurately and affectingly." I have often recalled this statement by Scorsese (which I'm citing here from memory) about viewing *Eyes Wide Shut* as the last-will-and-testament film of a filmmaker, Stanley Kubrick, who was one of the century's great virtuosos, and who grapples in his last work with seemingly minimalist scenes: a man and a woman conversing at length in their apartment, for example. With the "show-off calling card" genre of short films, one might think that it is much easier to de-

velop escape and avoidance strategies than it is to tackle the real difficulties of the cinematic creative process. The result is sometimes a short film that is hailed as "brilliant," and that is eventually a contender for festival prizes, but which contains no evidence that its author has learned anything in making it, other than how to avoid risk. Any pedagogy that includes an introduction to the creative process should be wary of this model, if it wants to stay its course.

This kind of short film brings to light a problem that, today, directly concerns the filmmaking projects of students in cinema departments. What will be evaluated when students make a film in an educational setting: the product or the process? Sometimes, the short films made by young people – unfortunately – resemble calling-card films, and are presented to the baccalaureate examiners for final marks with a strong belief of having done a good job.

One of the major dangers of making a short film in an educational setting is the associated flattening of the characters. Many characters in short films too closely resemble the two-dimensional thumbnails of a comic strip, are often defined by a few meagre traits that will be useful in a minutes-long screenplay, and too often lack the density of real life. There is no serious reason, however, that the characters in a short film should not be as real and as alive as the characters in a feature film. It's not a problem of scale: when a filmmaker knows how to film a character with substance and with a past, the character is living and breathing from the very first shot, even if the film says nothing about the contents of his current or past life. What's lacking, in the dominant model of short filmmaking, is the very idea that a character could have baggage, that the viewer might not know everything about him, that he might retain an element of mystery, that he could be assumed to have a larger existence than his short screenplay-bound lifetime.

Often similarly missing from the typical short film is the feeling of temporality, which should likewise not be a function of film format. It is possible to make a five-minute-long film in which time exists, in which you feel that the shots have a present tense, and that these shots were filmed in living time. In many short films whose aim is to demonstrate mastery, displaying their storyboarded shots as others exhibit their flexed muscles, time is often nonexistent or flattened. To tell, to signify, becomes the main objective, and time is crushed under the weight of a single-minded passion for enunciation. The length of the film makes no difference: you can make real cinema in a single shot just as there can be grace in a single good act, and just as there can be "bodybuilder" cinema in an hour and a half of vain and ungraceful efforts. The feeling of temporality and rhythm is derived from a musical attentiveness to the many rhythms that come into play in each shot, a kind of attention that is poorly adapted to a pure fixation on control. It is a small music that must be listened to, and that calls for the filmmaker to have the capacity to forget himself as the controlling subjectivity at certain moments in the creative process.

All of these elements, which often cause problems for short films, pose significant challenges in a pedagogical context. Films made in and for educational institutions are often "rigged" precisely as a result of this context, which we must nevertheless fully accept. These films rarely possess any real freedom – without which there can be no real creative process – because neither teachers nor students are able to take liberties. In an instructional setting, it is almost inevitable that students are asked to demonstrate mastery, and thus are perpetually in danger of producing "forced" cinema. How can we transform pedagogy so that what's important is that there is life in a shot, and so that it is not as easy to capture this life as it is to produce meaning? So that merely filming is not sufficient to guarantee that something will be truly inscribed onscreen? How can we make it clear that rhythm is the essence of cinema, and that characters must give the impression of being free, of escaping the pre-determined dictates of the screenplay, and of inventing or discovering their life in each shot?

The educator passes down tools for analysis and control, and thus ultimately for codification. But when these tools for control backfire against the very nature of what one is trying to teach, there is a great danger of betraying the very thing that one has loved in cinema, as do too many short films conceived as a means to an end and obsessed with efficiency. Nowadays I've come to believe that our students would do better to truly make a shot, sometimes, but as an intimate experience, rather than to make a twenty-minute film in which they have experienced nothing of what constitutes the true nature of the cinematic creative process.

Shooting a short segment of a longer "hypo-thetical" film can be more educationally bene-ficial that contorting oneself according to the castrating constraints of a short film in a form that might win the "audience prize" in a festi-val. The quality of the experience of making a film resides in a single question: have I really confronted cinema? Do I know a bit more, per-sonally, about my desire and my abilities in filmmaking after having had this experience? In a university where the students were able to di-rect little films, I came up with the strategy of asking them to shoot ten minutes of a feature-length film rather than a ten-minute short film. This changed everything: they had to think of a story that would hypothetically unfold over the course of a ninety-minute film, characters who would have to stay the course across the duration of a feature, and a temporality on this scale. The ten minutes to be filmed would preferably be selected from the middle of the film, were the film to be shot in full force, so to speak. In this way, students figured out how to film characters who were assumed to have an existence before and after the scenes being filmed. As a spectator, it's an easy experiment to compare five minutes excerpted from the middle of a feature film, and a five-minute short film: the density of real existence in every aspect of the film is, nine times out of ten, con-siderably richer in the excerpted clip. The lat-ter's power of imaginative evocation is incom-parable: what is not visible in the clip is none-theless mysteriously present, and carries deep resonances that are often absent from the short film. Nothing would prevent students from recounting the story of the entire movie, or handing out a written summary, when the clip is exhibited for parents or another audience. Thus each viewer will know that these three scenes ought to be experienced as a piece of a longer film. What's screened is presented as the result of a learning experience and not as a "finished product." The expectation, then, will no longer be based on the stereotypical notion of a short film that would be presented in com-petition or in a festival. As a result, this exercise might avoid the perennial plot-driven stories, the caricatural exaggerations of narrative ele-ments, the stereotypical characters with no backstory, and the inexistent treatment of tem-porality, which is sacrificed to mere narration. In this way, what's left out enriches what's left in.

FRAGMENT / WHOLE, IN PRACTICE

One of the major difficulties, in a pedagogy rooted in an introduction to practice, consists in the idea of the whole and the fragment that any cinematic production engages with.

The location scouting stage is symptomatic of this difficulty. Spontaneous naiveté entails choosing a location – for instance, "this partic-ular café" – because it seems to me to be per-fectly suited to the atmosphere that I need for my scene. The amateur or novice filmmaker risks discovering too late, after editing his film, that the atmosphere that had seduced him dur-ing scouting is totally absent from his scene.

This happens for a simple and obvious reason, but one whose obviousness the novice often only discovers as a result of disappointment and failure: in location scouting, when I enter a café, I have an overall perception of the atmosphere, the space as a whole, a certain emotion that it gives off, without breaking it down into its component parts (sounds, objects, colors, lights), which were, however, the things that instantaneously comprised my overall perception of this potential location. During the film shoot – though the simple fact that a film is being shot threatens to disturb this "natural" atmosphere, especially if someone yells "silence" to ensure that dialogue is picked up clearly – I will only capture a fraction of these components with the camera and the microphone, depending on the camera angles selected when I edit my scene and the microphone positions that are needed. After editing, a great many constitutive elements of the atmosphere perceived during scouting will be absent from the scene, and a new, unfamiliar café will appear, reconstituted by the partial sensations that I recorded from the real café. The café that has been filmed and edited together is always a *different* café, one which doesn't exist in reality. This, when it is not brought under control, can be the source of many disappointments.

In this, there are possibilities for simple exercises: each student, for example, could be instructed to capture, in three still shots, with a lens roughly corresponding to human vision (50mm with a 24x36 ratio), the general atmosphere of a place that offers an abundance of complex perceptions and sensations. If the same rule applies to everyone for the same place (a train station, for example, or a town plaza), a comparison of their individual efforts will prove to be thoughtful and profitable, with each student having had to confront the same difficulties as the other students whose results they are seeing.

Regarding what's left of a setting once the scene has cut it up into shots, one often encounters a major tension in the filmmaking process between *showing* and *telling*. When you scout a location, you perceive it as a space, a general atmosphere, precisely as decor, but when you cut up the scene that must unfold there, you most often do so as a function of the scene to be narrated, of its dramaturgy, as it were. The difficulty is always great – even for a professional filmmaker – in thinking about editing both in terms of the demands of "storytelling," of structuring relationships between the characters, of constructing meaning, and also as the decomposition-recomposition of a place, a space, an ambiance. In a café scene, for example, where the stakes involve jealousy (a boy seated at a table sees his girlfriend enter with a rival for her affections), the editing will undoubtedly be constructed along the axis connecting the watcher and the watched. It could be that along this axis, you never see the counter, for example, nor the corner filled with arcade games, and these blind spots for the film constitute an essential part of the atmosphere for which the café was chosen.

A poor solution – a bit "scholarly," in the worst sense of the term – too often involves including a shot of the whole space as an atmospheric "establishing" shot, before moving on to the montage whose only purpose is to construct the scene's dramatic meaning. It is more difficult, but virtually indispensable in terms of an apprenticeship, to convey the idea that editing is perpetually caught in a state of tension between these two requirements of *showing* and *telling*. One can imagine here, too, some beneficial exercises drawing on a single location and a single simple narrative premise, where each student must create a montage of four shots, taking into account both the narration and the reconstitution of the space at the same time. In order to tackle the issue of "real space / filmed space," according to the framework of *Le Cinéma, cent ans de jeunesse*, the following shooting exercise was proposed: starting with the decor and space of the school building, all entirely familiar to every one of the participants, each student (or small group of students) was required to "invent" a new space, constructed around a narrative scenario involving movement, a chase, and so on. The rule of the game was that the viewer, who would not be acquainted with the real locations (as is practically always the case for the viewer in cinema), would be able to mentally construct, on the basis of the connections between shots that are linked by the narrative logic, a spatial representation of the location, plausible and coherent, but absolutely false in relation to reality. This exercise allows students to understand, better than a long lecture

could, that filmed space across several shots in a preexisting location always creates, in editing, a different space out of this real space, and that this reconstituted space is, for the viewer, the only space that exists and the only one that matters.

This question of the whole and the fragment also comes up, crucially, in relation to the dramatic action itself. The concept of the shot and of editing is not "natural" for children, especially for young children, even if they are great consumers of films. Their "innocence" as viewers makes them perceive the succession of linked shots as a relatively continuous flow, even if they know perfectly well, otherwise, that there are differences between shots and differences in their sizes. But after all, classical cinema devised all of its rules for editing and linking shots in order to enhance the fluidity of the flow of shots and to make viewers – all viewers – forget the constitutive discontinuity of the film as much as possible. And even the most informed adult, who is intellectually conscious of the editing of films, lets himself be carried away by the flow of images from the moment he enters into the world of the film and its fiction. The regime of "I know better, but still…" is the only possible good system for the viewer, and his knowledge about film does not prevent him from turning back into an "innocent" viewer during the screening, at least the first time he sees a film, and to forget in some small way its discontinuity. No one, even the most informed viewers, can have an awareness of all the shots that make up a film, nor even a single sequence.

Here, again, there is a gulf between what students understand with regard to this question of the film's fragmentation into shots and what part of this knowledge they can mobilize when they begin trying their hand at the practice of filmmaking. The fact that they have worked on shot segmentation for certain sequences analyzed in class will have no bearing on the fact that the urge to cut will be more spontaneous as soon as they are in a position to make a film. Faced with a scripted narrative scenario, the first proposition from students, especially very young students, consists in placing the camera in a position from which it can see everything, and directing the scene in continuity in front of the camera. This is most often what's responsible for a scene that is incomprehensible for the viewer: the camera is too far away from the action, it's impossible to distinguish gestures and looks, the actors block one another from view, and often, because of the distance, the dialogues are nearly inaudible.

How can we help bring about the realization that cutting up a scene is necessary in order to render it visible, audible, and intelligible? Jean-Luc Lhuillier, a director of photography, worked with students at a professional high school for girls, who had little familiarity with cinema, to develop an utterly pragmatic method that seems to me to be much more valid, in terms of real apprenticeship, than the method of making students draw a storyboard in advance, before they've necessarily felt the need for it. First, Lhuillier let the group of students film the scene in the space, without intervening to help with problems of visibility and legibility created by this initial set-up, which is often very approximate and does not really take into consideration the camera's point of view. Then, he entrusts one student with a digital camera, telling her to take four photos of the scene, as though she wanted to tell the story with these four images. Once the photos have been taken while the "actors" were performing the scene, the students look at them as a group to see whether they allow an onlooker to see and comprehend the narrative. This is generally not the case, and they must then try to analyze why: because the camera was not in the right place, at the right distance and the right angle, but also because the positioning of the actors and the layout of the scene were not right, or because the actors performed the scene badly. They can then start over with the exercise after this critical stage, and little by little they will succeed, through trial and error and immediate analysis of the results, in achieving rapid improvements in placement, execution, and editing. The benefit of the digital camera (or the mini DV camera operated in photo mode, which amounts to the same thing) is obviously that the photos taken over the course of this introductory exercise cost nothing, and that students can see them and react to them instantaneously, as a group, on a television monitor. The still photo clearly has an advantage over the moving image, at this moment in the process, in that it requires the filmmaker to think through the segmentation of shots, and to reconsider with every image the question of point of view, camera angle, and distance.

FROM PRE-PRODUCTION TO SHOOTING

The misunderstood practice of making a storyboard can prove to be pedagogically disastrous when this tool ends up perverting the experience of being introduced to filmmaking practice in an effort to better cover up the fear associated with it. We must start by stating loudly and clearly that storyboarding is an uncommon practice in "true" cinema, where it is mostly of interest only for large productions requiring the construction of sets in the studio, or special effects, or just the presence of several crews. Under normal conditions, most filmmakers might occasionally make a few sketches of shots, but rarely arrive on set with all of their shots meticulously outlined in advance. Except in situations with burdensome constraints, a filmmaker who is beginning a day of shooting arrives on set with several basic ideas about his camera angles and how his scene will be cut, but decides at that moment, *in situ*, on the actual shot breakdown of the scene, the choice of camera angles and framings, as a function of the time available to him and the reality of the film shoot as it presents itself on that day.

It is best to learn how to first comprehend the scene as a whole, the space and its constraints, the major axes, the overall choices, before moving on to the shot-by-shot breakdown. No filmmaker initially thinks through a scene shot-by-shot.

The filmmaker's intelligence rests in this capacity for finding the right solutions for his mise-en-scène at the intersection of his preconceived idea of the scene to be filmed (the narrative "objective" of the scene, if you will, which make it necessary to the overall narrative) and the real conditions of this particular day of shooting. Those conditions range from weather to the actors' moods to the amount of time allotted to amass all of the shots that will constitute this scene. A good filmmaker must be capable of this dialectical flexibility between his imagined vision of the scene and the reality of the conditions of his mise-en-scène. Since the lovely constraint of cinema is the need to take reality into account every day and for every shot, the negotiation involved in this encounter is one of the major skills that is indispensable for any filmmaker.

The often spectacular appearance of storyboards that are published or included in DVD bonus features makes them utterly fascinating in the eyes of children and adolescents. But these storyboards are most often the product of professional designers who give them the seductive and prestigious air of a perfectly executed comic strip. A pedagogy concerned with storyboarding would assume a perfect mastery of drawing that children of eight or ten years couldn't be expected to have, with few exceptions. Indeed, the same is even true for adults. The filmmakers who are capable of drawing a publishable storyboard for themselves, as an autonomous graphic artwork, are very rare. There are great filmmakers, like Godard, whose films demonstrate representational power and visual inventiveness with each shot, but who are nonetheless mediocre at drawing, unlike an Eisenstein or a Fellini, who are perhaps brilliant exceptions.

The absurdity of using storyboards at a too-early age rests in the fact of asking a child to imagine a shot in advance, far away from the setting in which he will film it – a task which is already difficult, even for an adult – and to give form to this imagined image with an instrument, drawing, of which he is in poor command of the rules and techniques. To solve one problem, such a strategy would raise a second one. Then, at the film shoot, the major risk would be to want at all costs to execute the preconceived design while remaining closed to new and different options suggested by real conditions. How can a child imagine, in the classroom, the light that it will encounter on set? What filmmaker would not take into account, for his mise-en-scène and his framing, this light that makes his subject perceptible in the image?

In a pedagogy of creation, a storyboard only makes sense if it is regarded as one possible pre-formalization among others, and not necessarily as the best option, depending on the conditions of the film shoot and the nature of the project. The film needn't be its trace nor its execution. Incidentally, filmmakers more commonly use the floor plan of the scene, where the camera positions, the main angles chosen for filming, and the scene's blind spots, invisible onscreen, are all more globally visible than they would be in a storyboard.

The true intelligence behind what happens at a film shoot will never be located in an absurd respect for a storyboard, however perfect it might be, especially under the filmmaking conditions that would be present in an educational setting. What's at stake, in this question of storyboarding, is often the educator's fear, for which the storyboard acts as an anti-anxiety mechanism in the face of the black hole of decisions to be made urgently at the moment of shooting. The prestige enjoyed by the storyboard in the eyes of students is also cultivated by the media, thanks to images of the all-powerful creator "who already has everything in his head before beginning his film," and who carries sadistic perfectionism to an extreme in the execution of his own plan. Schools are not obligated to reinforce this wholly reductive image of the cinematic creative process, and they ought to suggest others.

There must be time allotted for "planning," where a filmmaker thinks through a scene's segmentation and shots, but it is imperative that he reserve some time for stewing over and thinking through the setting itself, before making decisions that will be definitively inscribed in the film. Jean Renoir endlessly repeated the view that in cinema, one must be passive before being active: "I think that's the number one rule in art, whatever art it may be. You must allow the elements of the act to conquer you. Afterward you may manage to conquer it, but first it has to conquer you. You have to be passive before you can be active."[55] The best attitude, when a crew of children arrive on set to shoot the scene that they have already thought through in class, is to begin by taking time to

55 Jean Renoir, *Renoir on Renoir: Interviews, Essays, and Remarks*, op. cit., p. 180.

look, to soak in what this location, this light, can bring anew to the preconceived idea that they've formulated for the scene. It can be a good tactic to ask students to look and listen in silence for several minutes, before doing anything. Only then can they begin to have the "actors" perform in this setting to see, again, what might improve on the initial idea that they had constructed as to the actors' positions and movements. Finally, rather than following the segmentation to the letter, shot by shot, as it was written on paper, they can usefully reconsider the major camera angles that will be used to film the scene, but which will take into account what could not have been *foreseen* and what constitutes the here-and-now of the shoot. Often the visualization conceived at this moment, on the set itself, is more useful than what the students had conceived abstractly in the classroom. None of what I'm describing has anything to do with any sort of "improvisation." Rather, it's simply the normal process of taking reality into account that must go into every cinematic act of creation, even the most meticulously planned most firmly pre-determined production. It's only by respecting these "listening" conditions of reality that the film shoot avoids being a mere simulation of creative practice.

TIME FOR THE SENSORIAL

The other sizable issue at stake during a film shoot is the indispensable awareness of everything that falls under the umbrella of perceptions and sensations, as much with regard to sounds as images. The pre-production process has taken into account the scene's segmentation and framings – that is, in the end, its form as a structure of meaning more than the perceptual substance of the shot. In school settings, there is a risk, if you restrict yourself to segmentation or to a *storyboard* (which would essentially determine the framing and point of view of every shot), of messing up everything in a cinematic shot that has to do with perception: the lighting, the materials, the internal rhythms of the actors' movements, the grain of the sound – in short, everything that has more to do with sensation than with meaning.

It is of the utmost urgency, if one truly wants to teach cinema as an art, to stop privileging the linguistic dimension to the detriment of this more sensitive approach. Walter Benjamin identified this sentiment, to which he fully subscribed, in a letter: "The primary objective of a truly *educational* museum must be to refine our perceptions."[56]

Today it has become especially necessary that the new tools for recording images and sounds no longer require us, technically, to ask basic questions about lighting, focus, and apertures that even the limitations of film stock, for instance, used to impose. With a miniature DV camera, the cameraman has at his disposal automatic mechanisms for adjusting the aperture and focus, a reliable digital method for directly

56 Letter regarding *Le Regard de Georges Salles*, in Walter Benjamin, *Ecrits français*, Bibliothèque des idées, NRF Gallimard, 1997.

recording sound, and above all a sensitivity that allows him to film in virtually any kind of light, even at night. All of these technical upgrades were obviously designed for use by the general public, by consumers who must, in all circumstances, obtain acceptable images and sounds without having had to consider the slightest question of aesthetic or technical choices in advance. These are obviously not the specifications of someone – a filmmaking instructor or professional, say – who wants to create an awareness of *creative choices*. The pedagogical deficiency inherent in the functionality of these new cameras is that there will always be a "visible" image, even if the students have not spent one second thinking about the lighting, where previously they would have been afraid of discovering, in the resulting footage, that the shot was too dark or too blurry and unusable in editing, and this fear would have more or less forced them to think through the question. The same is true with regard to focus: there will always be a "standard" focus, a clear area in the image, even if it was not considered nor chosen.

I am not in the least saying this to lament these technical advances whose pedagogical virtues are, on the whole, greater than the drawbacks. They must simply be taken into account by whoever is tasked with guiding students in their introduction to creative practice: from now on the responsibility is his, and his alone, to permanently maintain certain standards with respect to everything that constitutes the perceptible visual and sonic material of the shots his students film. The new tools

will quickly absorb many of the inhibitions and fears that teachers experience surrounding the technical aspects of teaching filmmaking, but will in turn require from the adult, whether a visiting speaker or a teacher, a still greater vigilance towards the purpose of this practical experience. This is where a professional practitioner working in image- or sound-recording, invited into the classroom as a guest speaker, can bring an invaluable sensitivity to "refine the perceptions" of the students with regard to a lighting choice, an interplay of colors, a sonic texture, on the basis of a value system that is particular to his craft, and which can serve to awaken in the group a greater perceptive intensity. When I talk of the group, I'm referring to the one that consists of the students *and* the teachers, for even a film teacher (teaching an elective course in film studies, for example) has much to learn from a professional man or woman who unpacks all of the finer points of his or her perception of a shot or a scene, which daily experience has honed to an extreme degree, and which can be contagious. I remember a very moving talk by Nestor Almendros that made visible, with slides of photograms and paintings by Caravaggio, the workings of light and shadow in cinema. Far from inducing any technical intimidation, this great cinematographer gave each listener the feeling that light was, above all, a matter of sensitive choices. This is obviously the best outcome you could hope for from a professional guest speaker in the classroom: that he would convey the technical translation of his craft following a sensitization to the very nature of the materials with which he works: sound, light, costume, setting, and so on.

THE ATTRACTIONS OF COLLABORATIVE CREATION

The crucial question, and the only one that really matters, in the end, is the following: can one have a true experience of the creative process in the classroom, in an institutional framework? Under what conditions?

Filmmaking practice, in a school setting, is always in danger of dodging the individual experience of the creative act, without which there can be no real creation.

In pedagogy, we have too often sung the praises of cinematic creation as collaborative creation. Everything is declared to be for the best – in the best of all possible pedagogical worlds – when each student is supposed to have found his place in this supposed "community" while filming, where the virtues of socialization are reputedly immediate and quasi-automatic. This myth has been hard to combat. It must first be said that a true filmmaking crew has nothing in common with a gentle anarchistic utopia where each person harmoniously finds his place according to his expertise and his creative appetite. It is a configuration based primarily on efficiency and productivity, military-style, ultra-hierarchical, with the chief technician in each department (image, sound, set design, etc.) being responsible for his men and the quality of their work. The famous conversation of creativity is in fact often limited to a conversation between "generals": essentially, the director, the director of photography, and the actors. A mechanic or an electrician rarely provides their artistic opinion about the film or the shot being filmed, and it's rare that anyone asks them for it. Standard professional cinematic creation has nothing to do with community, even if it requires the most harmonious possible teamwork.

The pseudo-collaborative film shoots in schools too often reproduce – imitating the model of a "real" set without knowing it – hierarchies that are not professional (and for good reason), but which are rather assignments that have already been inscribed in the class group as a microcosm of the social group: the prettiest girl will naturally be an actress or interviewer, the alpha-male will direct, the shy thoughtful student will be script girl, the smart boy will operate the camera, and so on. An introduction to filmmaking practice obviously makes no sense (in terms of real educational value) unless it modifies these patterns that have been ingrained in students' heads since they first played in the schoolyard, as Claire Simon's film *Récréation* masterfully showed us. What kind of creative experience can be had by a boy or girl who, being accustomed to taking as few risks as possible because of failures already endured in class, will choose the most "cushy" and menial work station, where he will be the least "exposed"? For everyone does not have the same part to play in the creative process – far from it – within the division of labor that makes up a film crew, even in the classroom, and it's useless to pretend to believe this, unless you intend to reproduce this division of labor in all good faith.

If an introduction to creative practice has a collective meaning, in the school system, it can only serve to redistribute somewhat the cards that have already been overplayed, in the classroom and in the surrounding society, between good and bad students, the strong and the weak, those who speak out and those who wouldn't dare to, the dominant and the dominated, the "legacy heirs" and the culturally impoverished, those who "have a future" and those who "have no future." I am wary of examples that seem a bit too miraculous, like the canonical story of the autistic child who started speaking and communicating thanks to a filmmaking experience, but I am convinced, from having often seen direct proof, that the experience of working on the production of a film can be the opportunity and the trigger, with certain students who have already been assigned a status and an expectation of failure by the institution, for a restoration of self-confidence – provided that the new "deal" that the practical learning experience should represent is not shirked as a result of the reproduction of roles already established in the classroom. This is not an easy thing to ensure, even with the best intentions on the part of the teacher. When all of the conditions of vigilance and attentiveness are combined, an introduction to filmmaking practice can indeed make it possible for certain students who are underperforming or falling behind to "regain control" thanks to this new activity, to reveal to everyone, peers and teachers alike, qualities that had until then never found expression, and to alter their own self-image, for themselves and for

others. Approaching cinema as an art, if it is done coherently throughout, involves the teacher taking stock of personal qualities other than those which find expression normally in the school system. There is a different form of intelligence, of creative ability, a different mode of self-expression that can be revealed through a practical filmmaking experience, which has the great virtue of opening very wide the field of new possibilities for each student involved. This field can encompass everything from one's ability to "be an actor" to one's ability to frame actors in movement, not to mention the ability to write rhythmic, lively, and well-timed dialogues, or to skillfully construct a piece of decor with pieces of string. Few kinds of artistic practice open such a large number of new doors to those for whom schools have already closed so many. The visiting guest speaker, whose values are different and who knows nothing, when he arrives, of the hierarchies and segregations already in place in the classroom, can play an invaluable symbolic role by detecting, according to his own criteria, new skills in certain children who had until then shied away from any legitimization.

If an educator does not want to be too hasty in rating the artistic abilities of a child or an adolescent in accordance with the rhetorical skills that are already recognized and taught in schools, namely writing and speech, the educator must know how to preserve an element of the unsaid: art is a way of speaking differently, not always with words, and not necessarily according to rational logic. The teacher who demands that the student justify all of his creative choices, rationally and with words, is fulfilling his role as a teacher, but risks diminishing the creative act by eliminating the essential element of intuition, of risks taken in the silent solitude of a decision, of engagement with the subject. There is one part of the self that finds expression through the act of creation, and which is precisely the part that cannot do so by resorting to deductive logic and a kind of discourse that reigns supreme in ordinary classroom activities. Ignoring this part of the self, or denying it, once again diminishes the act of creation by taking away something that is constitutive of it: intuition, reflex, inspiration. It's often *afterward*, when success has validated their efforts, that certain students gain access to the power of speech. They must first regain their self-confidence through action.

THE INDIVIDUAL MOMENT OF PRACTICAL EXPERIENCE

It must be said again: what really constitutes the creative process is as solitary in cinema as it is in the other arts. Solitude and risk-taking are at the heart of the act of creation, in cinema as much as in painting or literature. Even in the context of a sixty-person crew, the director is absolutely the only one who holds in his mind an idea of the film to come, and who wagers that the partial choices that he is in the process of making, in the middle of all this agitation and all these constraints, will be validated in a few weeks or a few months when the film will begin to exist as a totality. Cinema is an art of

the "too-late," where the element of gambling in the moment is the strongest there is. The filmmaker's special talent, which is often linked to his personal charisma, is to inspire in all of the members of the crew a diffuse emotional image of what the film should be, to lead through contagion more than through explanation, in order to create a certain harmony in each crew member's idea of the film that the director has in mind, and of which he has entrusted a piece to each person in the crew. This piece might be more or less visible, depending on whether it involves, for example, the work of the actor, who attracts the attention of every viewer; the work of the cinematographer, which only a portion of the audience will notice; the work of the sound mixer, of which only a tiny minority will be aware; or the work of the driver tasked with the extremely sensitive and delicate job of pushing the dolly, which no one thinks about – but the film as a finished artistic object will be made up of the traces left by these many tasks. The harmony or discord of the whole will often depend on the climate that the filmmaker will have succeeded, or not, in spreading around himself and his project, at each stage and with each collaborator in the film's creation.

At the highest level, in primary or secondary school, it is important that each student, individually, be confronted at least once with full and total responsibility for a creative task, with all of the choices, the decision-making authority, the risks, the excitement, and the shivers that it brings with it. And there's no need for each student to make "his own" film, which would obviously be impractical in a classroom group context. But it is necessary to preserve at all costs, regardless of the concrete pedagogical circumstances, time for both individual creativity and group creativity.

At some point, each student must have total and exclusive responsibility for a creative task: filming one, two, or three shots, or splicing two shots together. But it's essential that he should resolve all the decisions on his own, that he personally takes all the risks, while following the rules of the game that everyone is playing, but without having to justify himself to anyone while the creative process is underway. The time for exchange will come later, when each student will screen his shot, or his montage made from three shots filmed by other students. At that moment, the child will not be called upon to rate or evaluate his work in relation to the work of other people, but merely to watch attentively how the others respond to it, and the benefits are great when another student has also been confronted with the same choices, following the same rules and with the same margin for artistic liberty.

I had the opportunity to experiment for years, in the framework of *Le Cinéma, cent ans de jeunesse*, trying out a pedagogical strategy that continues to prove its worth. It involves extending the practical creative learning experience across two stages.

The first stage is dedicated to introducing a major area of inquiry in cinema – for instance, the distinction between real space and filmed space. This introduction is launched "from both ends": film analysis and filmmaking exercises. On the side of analysis, students watch and compare film sequences, selected from across the history of cinema, that bring into play, in an illuminating way, the question of space constructed by the film. The understanding and exchange around this question are thus not born out of a discourse imposed by the teacher or the guest speaker, but rather, first, from observations and comparisons of film excerpts.

At the same time, on the side of practical instruction, we propose two or three exercises – adaptable depending on the age level of the class, their degree of familiarity with cinema, and the concrete conditions of production – that allow each student to tackle the same question in a simple manner. I have already put forward two or three examples of such "exercises," where each student is called upon to suggest a simple rule: for example, to imagine three shots that would believably stitch together three spaces in the school that are, in reality, separated and not connected.

It is only in the second stage, when each student will have filmed, edited, and presented his three shots to the other students, that they will begin to work on one or several group productions where each person will learn to assume "his" partial responsibility in a team effort.

Sometimes, one shot is enough to provide a strong and unforgettable experience of the cinematic creative process, if the conditions of the experience are carefully and rigorously defined and guided. An experiment implemented in 1995, under the same framework of *Cinéma, cent ans de jeunesse*, supplied the most beautiful evidence in support of this claim: a film composed of some sixty shots, each a minute long, filmed in color Super 8 film with sound by children and young people ranging in age from 10 to 18 years, spread out all over France.[57] Every participating class had the opportunity, at the start, to discover on a big screen the "pictures" filmed by the Lumière brothers, and to soak up their spirit and their apparatus. Then, each student selected and scouted the location, the date and time at which he wanted to film his "Lumière shot," without any instruction other than to respect the conditions that were imposed at the birth of cinema: a minute-long still shot, with no possibility of taking it back. Each student then left to make his shot, to try out his chosen location and time, accompanied by a filmmaking professional, the teacher, and some "assistant" classmates. It had to be seen to be believed: the seriousness and the gravity of the moment where they had to decide to turn on the camera, the agony and the hopefulness with respect to everything that could go well or go poorly for *their* shot over the course of this fateful minute, more intense than any other, when the film was rolling.

Cinema is always youthful when it truly takes as its starting point the gesture upon which it was built, when it returns to its roots.

When someone takes a camera and trains it on reality for a minute, with a fixed frame, in a state of extreme attentiveness to everything that will occur, holding one's breath in the face of all that's sacred and inexorable in the fact that the camera captures the fragility of an instant, with the grave sentiment that this minute is unique and will never again be recreated in all of time, cinema is born again for that person as it was on the first day a camera ever filmed. When a person is engaged in what is inherent in the cinematic act, he is always the first filmmaker, from Louis Lumière to a young man or woman today. Making a shot is to already be at the heart of the cinematic process; to discover that there is, in the raw act of capturing a minute of the world, all the power of cinema; and above all, to understand in return that the world is always surprising, never entirely what one expects or envisions, that it often has more imagination than the person filming it, and that cinema is always stronger than the person making it. This apparently minuscule act of making a shot, if it's guided by an adult who is respectful of the feelings of the child carrying it out, brings into play the marvelous humility that belonged to the Lumière cameramen, but also the sacredness that a child or an adolescent can bring to a "first time" taken very seriously, as a decisive inaugural experience.

---

57 *Jeunes lumières*, 60 minutes, 35mm film, produced by *Le Cinéma, cent ans de jeunesse* and Agat Films et Cie, 1995.

Alejandro Bachmann

"To Talk and Write about Films and to Teach Cinema are the Last and Only Forms of Resistance Against Consumption and Amnesia"

A Conversation with Alain Bergala

ALEJANDRO BACHMANN: Fourteen years have passed since the first publication of *The Cinema Hypothesis*, in French. Having just re-read the book I was astonished in how many ways it shows a sensibility for the state of our culture as a whole and the things to come – with regard to the relationship of commercial cinema and "all the rest" as well as to the possibilities of the DVD or the Internet as tools for film education. Looking back, how do you feel about the impact the book had and in how far would you have approached things differently writing in 2016, if at all?

ALAIN BERGALA: In general, *The Cinema Hypothesis* anticipated the next 15 years quite precisely, especially the role of the DVD. When I suggested to the Secretary of State for Education in 2000 to produce new educational tools in the form of DVDs there were practically no DVD players in classrooms and many people in the ministry did not believe in that idea. It was a bet on the future and I was not absolutely sure that I would win it. My choice had not been motivated by technological reasons but primarily by pedagogical ones. The DVD allowed for a pedagogy of fragments, for putting fragments in relation with each other which seemed seminal when it came to teaching cinema. Since then, I have never felt the need to abandon this

idea of a comparative method. In our current situation, and looking at how we relate to cinema today, it actually seems more sensible than ever before.

The biggest change since 2000 concerns the way we see films and the way we see excerpts of films. By now we can talk of an atomisation and nomadisation of cinema. The atomisation refers to the fact that there is a very wide range of films and film excerpts available online – through sites such as YouTube, Daily Motion and Vimeo – where you can find a seemingly endless amount of film excerpts of different kinds, not taking into account the often inferior formats, sound and image quality, of course. The nomadisation is triggered by the multiplication of devices on which we can see films, such as computers, tablets and smartphones. This availability is totally scattered and anarchistic. It is time to think of a pedagogy of cinema via YouTube. I am currently working on just that.

BACHMANN: In having taught cinema to children and students myself for a couple of years I have been strongly influenced by the ideas and concepts you outline in this book. I was lucky to have the German translation of the text available, which was published in 2006 thanks to the efforts of Bettina Henzler and

Winfried Pauleit. The present English translation is intended to spread your ideas to an even broader group of film educators. The notion of "translation" thus becomes not only a matter of spoken (or written) language but one of cultural context: Writing as a cinephile in France goes hand in hand with a very strong cinema culture; do you think there could be a problem in other countries where people might decide to work with your method, as far as a certain lack of cinema culture is concerned – where an appreciation of the value and importance of that art form may not be as fully established as in France? Is there something that could be "lost in translation"?

BERGALA: The pedagogy I suggested in my book is first and foremost based on young people's direct experience of seeing films and excerpts. Before anything else, this experience is very personal and intimate. It happens between the film and the person seeing it and is not necessarily dependent on the cultural context in which these films were made. My experience in working with children from countries ranging from Brazil to Japan has shown that it is basically independent of a certain cinema culture in this or that country. Young Brazilians have as much to say about the comparison of three films from, let's say, Iran, France and Italy as young Frenchmen or children from Portugal. That is why it was always central to my work to make sure to choose films and film excerpts from all countries and cultural contexts. The cinema inhabits its own territory, it is a world devoid of nationalism. I am sad to say and nevertheless think that a young

Frenchman today, even though he was born into a nation with a strong cinema culture, will hardly know anything about it, it will leave no real impression on him. An encounter with cinema in his French classes might help to change this a little bit.

BACHMANN: I fully agree insofar as the beauty of cinema, and – ideally – of any other art form is that it does not depend on national contexts, that it is, as Vertov would have put it, a "universal language." I was rather referring to the implementation of a certain vision of how cinema could be taught in schools: When I read your text, I always imagined that it must be relatively easy to convince French educators, as they surely have a clear understanding of the role and importance of cinema. In many other countries cinema as an art form does not have a comparable status and it might be harder to convince people that it should be treated with this quite radical approach within the school system. If most of the teachers have grown up with an idea that the arts have little to do with cinema, it will be harder to convince them to teach cinema along the lines you are suggesting.

BERGALA: I am fully aware of the difficulties to convince those teachers for whom cinema is not an art form but a way of communication or purely entertainment. But believe me, this is also the case with a majority of teachers in France. The best solution is to organize little events that serve as an introduction, a point of entry, in which one has to bring the teachers into contact with films of indisputable quality. It is a matter of literally convincing them that the artistic quality of film is in every way comparable to that of painting or music. And I really believe in the power of contagion, that a truly convinced and enthusiastic person can "convert" many others – all the teachers of a school, for example. I have seen it happen a number of times: a passionate teacher working in a secondary or primary school begins to shape a team around him- or herself over the years, consisting of people who were not convinced at the start and who have become enthusiastic once they themselves have made the experience of coming into contact and discovering this art form.

BACHMANN: While *The Cinema Hypothesis* seems to be primarily a book about teaching cinema, it also feels like a book about cinema as a whole, as a statement of someone who has a deep appreciation of or love for that art form. Was it intended to function in both ways? Can one actually write a book about teaching cinema without talking about one's own views of, one's very personal passion for cinema?

BERGALA: I feel that any form of arts education is absolutely dependent on the taste and personal choice of the person acting as a teacher or initiator to truly hand on the love for the art form in question. We have all had teachers who transmitted to us the love of reading – by pointing out ("This is what I like about it") and through a form of contagion: The teacher's enthusiasm for a work which he or she loves and of which you feel that it touches him or her on a personal level is a powerful form of communication. This calls for a far more personal commitment compared to what I would call a classical form of education, where the educator is basically "protected" by his objective knowledge. For a *passeur* it is not about forcing one's choices or predilections onto others but rather about communicating the personal significance of a certain work of art and make it perceptible. The student who has felt an adult's or teacher's passion and joy in relation to a film can then choose very different films from his own life or the cultural context of his generation. It is first and foremost the passion in one's love of cinema and the personal joy that it evokes which we have to pass on. And this can only happen through individuals *and* films which are pointed out as desirable. The internet will be very helpful for cinema education, but it will never be able to replace the human contact between an adult and a student.

BACHMANN: This very much reminds me of what Jacques Rancière says in *The Ignorant Schoolmaster* – that one has to trigger the student's interest to learn, to see, to get involved by making him or her *want* something. And one way to do this is to show him or her why *I* want something, why something is important to *me*, how it touched me. Still, if I look at the concept of education in contemporary school systems, I am not overly optimistic that this form of teaching, which aims at transferring a passion, can be implemented. Education nowadays seems to be understood as acquiring certain skills and tools that one can "use" in a completely functional manner. This again makes me wonder if schools are the right places for this form of film education? The sort of film education we put into practice at the Film

Museum, for example, takes place in a cinema, away from school. I often feel that this gives me a certain freedom to talk differently about film. There seems to be a freedom outside of the school that allows you to perform education differently. Do we need to bring film into the school or should we not try to bring the schools to the cinema – into a different context, an ideal setting in terms of its darkness, its technical *dispositif*, and into a space where one is allowed to think differently, to trigger a form of education that gives more justice to an appreciation of art?

BERGALA: Absolutely, the ideal would be to teach cinema in those institutions devoted to cinema, in which the conditions are perfect and where one is free from the constraints of the educational system. But I fear that this would limit the number of young people with access to these privileges at these places – such as the Austrian Film Museum or the Cinémathèque Française, which are mostly located in big cities. The cinema education project that we wanted to implement with Jack Lang was to be relevant for the entire country, in all regions, all cities, in the countryside, where you basically have no cinemas at all. I was heavily attacked by those who claimed I would kill the cinemas and that it was a downright criminal act to produce the DVD series *L'Eden cinéma*. But it was important to us to enable every teacher with an urge to give an introduction to cinema to do so in his or her classroom. So while the classroom is surely not the ideal space to approach cinema it is nevertheless the most democratic place there is. And experience has shown that children or teenagers have discovered their love for and taste in cinema – a taste quite distinct from their social or geographic context – precisely because they encountered it in school.

But we do have an institution called *École et cinéma* in France that meets what you are suggesting: Students leave the school and go to the nearest cinema to watch films. To have this institution is of central importance, 10,000 schools and 1300 cinemas spread across the country are part of it. It has become an essential structure for the encounter of young people with cinema. But without the cooperation between the schools and these cinemas the project would have never seen the light of day. The solution might be found in alliances of this kind. But I still believe that art, if brought to school under the right circumstances, can change the school itself as well as those who work within it. The teachers who, in their classes, put into practice an introduction to cinema, are enjoying it; they enter into a relationship with their students which is quite different from the one usually structuring institutionalized learning.

There is a formula that I frequently quote: "only desire truly initiates learning." To me, this is now, more than ever, the main problem of what we call education. Serge Daney once said that on the day you have to force students to watch a film that you offer to them, it will be better to refrain from teaching cinema completely. I think he was right. One could never force anyone to learn anything, if he or she did not have that desire to learn it. That is the main problem with the educational system in France today: the breach between that which is made desirable to everyone through communication, the internet, the well-calibrated goods of consumption and that which everyone has to discover through his or her own desires. Education should provide both the time and the circumstances for everyone to discover his or her own desires. That fight is a long way from being won.

BACHMANN: In an early chapter of the book you reflect on institutions and the role they play in our education – singling out the school and cinema as the ones that were most important to you, in your own biography. Ever since, your own work as an educator of film has been closely connected to institutions, both in your work at Sorbonne Nouvelle and the Cinémathèque française. In the same breath, you also note that institutions tend to absorb any potential of being a place where one is confronted with otherness or alterity over the course of time. Do you see this tendency at the Cinémathèque française as well and if not, how do you think they avoided this trajectory? Do you feel that your educational work in the institution was always an effort to preserve the friction it can potentially offer?

BERGALA: The problem with institutions is that they tend to normalise, to homogenise and thus reduce the singularity of the works as well as the individual reactions towards them. At its core, every institution is afraid of everything that is too personal, too emotional and too unregulated with regard to the relationship between adult and child. Therefore, one often

has to begin by educating the institution. The most threatening aspect for the flourishing of such a kind of pedagogy is the educators' fear to lose control. But they can learn quite quickly that these fears are not entirely reasonable. On the contrary, they can begin to understand that that which is set free inside the children and teenagers in return triggers a passion to learn and express oneself. Institutions such as the Cinémathèque française are often far less prone to censoring than the national educational system because they carry less of an obligation towards students and their parents. It is all very delicate depending on each individual situation, but it can also create more freedom and satisfaction for the teacher in his work and in his or her relationship with the students. Institutions are afraid of any form of otherness that threatens their coherence. But nowadays – this is true for France, in any case, where the coherence of any school class is already in peril due to the social diversity, the diversity of origins and of families – the otherness of a work of art, of a film can become an occasion for exchange instead of withdrawal into one's own community. Otherness is something that each person experiences as engimatic and puzzling. The work of art stands apart from social discrimination that is at the centre of most school subjects. In the face of the artwork's otherness, of the unknown, we understand that everyone is the same.

BACHMANN: A movement that has definitely gained more force in the last couple of years is the digitization not only of contemporary films but also of film heritage, which is now not only available on DVDs or BluRays but has also entered the cinema space. From the perspective of the institution I work for this is regarded as a problematic development, as the loss of a film's material characteristics and its original *dispositif* goes hand in hand with a loss of an historical unterstanding of film as such. I find this question interesting and relevant especially with regard to your fascination for the pedagogical potentials of the DVD which you praised for making films available and its potential to bring fragments of different films into a dialogue with each other. While I agree with your remarks, I also wonder if teaching an understanding of and a sensibility for the material realities of analogue film should also have been part of film education, in order to grasp more of that medium's dimensions which cannot really be seperated from each other?

BERGALA: This is an essential question today and will become even more so in the time to come. Digital technology is about to occupy the entirety of cinema's terrain, from the production of film to its exhibition and preservation. But in 2016 the central question is not one of the storage medium but one of the *dispositif* in which we encounter a film: There is no crucial difference in terms of quality between a decent digital projection and the projection of an analogue print. And analogue film is in the process of disappearing rapidly, with the exception of heritage institutions. Most cinemas in France have completely gotten away with this changeover, which creates the problem of how to show films that have not yet been digitized. It has become much harder to program a retro-

spective outside of the state-funded institutions. Nevertheless, the significant change is to be found in an ever-widening gap between the *dispositif* of the cinema space (to sit with other spectators in darkness with an obligation to watch the film in its entirety and its own temporality) and the ways of watching film excerpts on nomadic screens, tablets, computers (jumping from one clip to the next in a state of impatience and with a lack of concentration while looking at yet another screen or doing something else). Random zapping or channel-hopping has nothing in common with creating relationships between excerpts in the way I am proposing. The main hazard of surfing the internet is that there is no point of reference that allows one to identify oneself with what one has just seen. Everything flows into an undifferentiated current where images have neither an origin nor a category, where cinema drowns in the midst of all the other images. Thus, I feel what is needed is a pedagogy of the projection *dispositif* more than a pedagogy of film.

BACHMANN: One of the potentials of the DVD is, as you have eloquently outlined in the book, that it allows us not only to work with fragments or excerpts of films but also to put them in relation to each other – we thus understand cinema as a dialogue, where each film potentially interacts with other films. I absolutely agree with this potential and it chimes with how I mostly work when I teach cinema. But in the last couple of years, I have also begun to wonder: Isn't the way we are using fragments very much in line with how younger people perceive films in general? Platforms like

YouTube or social networks like Facebook are dominated by a fragmentary representation of filmic works. What younger people seem less accustomed to is to watch a whole film, to take the time to spend two hours of their time on one single film. For me this raises the question if our didactic approach – working with fragments – might not be too similar to what young people are already used to. In how far can we create a stronger experience of alterity through the didactic tools we use to teach cinema?

BERGALA: You are right: The dominant mode of film consumption of young people nowadays is through excerpts, or "clips," as they are called and it has become a rare thing to see a film in its entirety, with the exception of those American blockbusters that have been designed specifically to be consumed by young people. Zapping creates impatience and distraction. On facebook a two-minute clip is already too long, as it encourages the teenager to switch to the next one. This is a practice that creates excitement and a form of being intoxicated by rapid circulation, but a "clip" is not an excerpt. The word "excerpt" points to the fact that this is a part taken from the body of the work as a whole. The "clip" is a small form, quick, autonomous and in no way relating back to the film as a whole. In internet traffic one clip chases the other and no memory is constructed with regard to that which one has seen. Cinephilia was the opposite. It was about creating connections between the films and constructing a cinema memory in that process. There is a tendency to say – even among so called "respectable" researchers and scientists –

that no teacher is needed because all of cinema can be found on the net. I find this to be a lazy, demagogic and irresponsible way of thinking, a form of populist pedagogy that is currently spreading. It means to resignate and put down the role of adults in the education of a younger generation.

A truly pedagogic application of excerpts has no relation whatsoever to zapping. The chosen excerpts are interconnected and these connections have been thought of by someone with a memory of cinema – the *passeur*. Without these thoughts and ideas the excerpts amount to nothing. And it is important nowadays to not only show excerpts but films in their entirety, may that be in the classroom or the cinema, where you have to watch the whole film without being distracted by other things. If one manages to achieve such a thing one will discover that young people enjoy it and will want to see other films in their entirety, although this urge has originated from excerpts.

BACHMANN: One central element to your approach of teaching cinema is to include the process of creation into our analysis and to not see them as different realms – theory and praxis. While I also tend to not differentiate between theory and praxis, I always asked myself if you opted for this combination on the basis of a specific quality in cinema that asks for this approach, or if you would see it as a general approach towards art education: In other words, do you also think that painting should be taught by looking, experiencing and reflecting on paintings as well as actually taking a brush into one's hand and start painting?

Would we also gain a deeper understanding of literature if we were asked to write a story as well as to read and reflect? Or does cinema lend itself to this approach because it differs from the other arts in one central aspect?

BERGALA: I think that – to answer your question – cinema is an art to itself. The reason for this is quite simple. Contrary to literature, painting or music cinema is "a written language of reality," as Pier Paolo Pasolini called it. And from its earliest childhood a person does not need to acquire any particular language to understand reality. It does not have to translate into another language (such as words in literature, artificial colours in painting, notes in music) what it perceives of reality in order to film it. Painting, writing, or making music asks for the command of a cultural code. To shoot a "Lumière minute" it is sufficient to position a machine at the site one has chosen, to frame what one wants to show, to choose where the shot is to begin and to press record. Jean-Luc Godard said that cinema is the art of childhood. It is without doubt the art form most closely related to childhood.

BACHMANN: What you are saying also brings up Raymond Bellour's concept of "The Unattainable Text" – the idea that film cannot be quoted the way a written text can be quoted, because it is an art form that articulates itself in time and through images and sounds. And once we start talking about cinema, once we use words, we have to transform what we see and hear into what we want to say or write – an act of translation. In the last couple of years, the "video essay" has become more and more

popular, and there are quite brilliant and challenging examples by critics and scholars such as Kevin B. Lee, Catherine Grant or Chloé Galibert-Lainé. In a way these people are making films (they are creating moving images) about cinema, often articulating their passion for cinema and combining it with a close analysis of certain shots, a montage sequence, a small moment that touches them. Would the making of video essays fall into what you call "the creative process" and in how far would this differ from going out and shooting a "Lumière minute"?

BERGALA: One has to distinguish between two categories of filmed essays about cinema. The first category is the classical model, where the video is a pure illustration of the preceding theoretical analysis. The shots one quotes are only there to prove the truth of what the words of the commentary say. And I have often seen that one can say almost anything, even prove things that are not true about certain shots or images if you use a convincing voice-over. This model has been the dominant mode of pedagogic or didactical essays on cinema. It is always in danger of drowning the film in the commenting voice while it pretends to be objective in its quotations. It is a comforting model but prone to dogmatism.

The second model is more varied and creative. It is the one where the director experiments, invents, truly searches for new ideas about the film he is analysing. He does so while he is making the film essay, departing from his own work with the images and sounds of the film. That is the only category worthy of being called "film essay." If it really is an essay, it does not follow any blueprint, its form has to be found time and time again in relation to the film or the topic it deals with. Jean-Luc Godard is the true master of this model of film essays and his *Histoire(s) du cinéma* is the monumental trial in that respect.

At the 52. Mostra Internationale del Nuovo Cinema in Pesaro, Adriano Aprà put together a retrospective of what he called the "critofilm", which was accompanied by a mesmerizing e-book surrounding this question of filmic essays on cinema.

The film essay is a genre that requires a certain intellectual and artistic maturity and a refined mastery of montage. I am not sure whether this can easily be done with children in pedagogical conditions because it asks for an individualistic and solitary work of experimentation and a lot of time. But one could surely find simpler forms of reflecting on cinema through experimentation, for example by determining, extracting and organizing certain shots.

BACHMANN: In your approach, you strongly emphasize the need to confront young people with films that you would consider as true cinematic works, and you use the following definition: Cinema becomes an art when our emotions and thoughts are provoked by a form, by a rhythm that only exists in or through cinema. You place this approach in opposition to a form of education that wants to teach young people to become aware of the manipulative powers of cinema, often showing them "bad cinema" as a "warning" example. This reminded me of

something that Jean Douchet once said, namely that if a film is art, its qualities cannot be articulated through language but have to be made comprehensible by talking about films that are not art: We get an understanding for what art is in cinema by establishing a relation to films that are not. For me, this raises the question of the role of language in the process of film education. What sort of language does a film educator have to develop to teach cinema, to talk about things that cannot really be grasped by language?

BERGALA: I never really believed in an encounter with cinema through bad films in order to contrast them with so-called good films. It always seems easier to start with a film that was made to be consumed without further complications, a film that is pre-digested in comparison to a film that is the result of a truly creative process. True works of art always oppose easy consumption. They ask for a form of trust and goodwill on the part of the spectator so that he or she may be rewarded at a later stage, when the work has found its place in the head. The joy is less immediate but far more sustainable and it can truly construct something within the teenager who is yet to grow up. But he or she must be acquainted with the one who will point out this film and show it and he or she must hope that there will be something worthwhile and enriching in it.

I do not think that language is insufficient to talk about cinema just because the emotion or thought we try to express has originally been triggered by cinema. An emotion that we cannot talk about cannot be shared, even if we are aware that words will not sufficiently describe that emotion in its entirety. But something of the specificity of a film nevertheless seeps through, through the words. My years as a critic with the *Cahiers du cinéma* have taught me that one can sometimes articulate the singularity of a certain film through words – through hard work. One can achieve this through the filter of emotions that one experienced when seeing it. But it is really a matter of working on the words. I have always believed, and still do, in the virtue of description – of a shot, a gesture, a scene. To describe is always already to interpret and to share with others what has touched us in a certain moment of a film. For children this is a task that comes quite naturally as they love to describe what they have seen.

The extraction of images from films on a computer is very easy to do nowadays, so one could imagine that children articulate their own approach towards a film without having to use words, simply by taking screenshots and arranging them. This personal approach has the advantage that it can be shared with others, especially if they were also asked to articulate themselves through these "personal screenshots."

Over the years, I have often encountered a process of emotional education that takes place outside of language and can nevertheless be shared, is not confined to be captured within one person. In some of the films that children and teenagers made during *Le Cinéma, cent ans de jeunesse* one can trace the imprint of an excerpt which they had seen at the very beginning of the year, at the time when one would approach the topic of that year. These imprints where neither an imitation nor a quote but a form of profound and direct, not necessarily verbal impregnation between seeing and making. Something of a film they had seen had an emotional impact on them and mysteriously finds its way into the film they shoot themselves. It is a form of pedagogy of impregnation taking place outside of language that is hardly ever put into practice. During my studies on Jean-Luc Godard I have often found these impregnated shots which stem from shots he had seen in other films a long time ago and that he was not consciously aware of at the time.

BACHMANN: You specifically emphasize that cinema education is not equivalent with an education in television because these two media inhabit very different realms of the moving image. Since 2002 the television landscape has changed quite radically, especially with the advent of a wide range of TV series that are often praised for their cinematic qualities: US series like *The Wire* or *Deadwood* come to mind, in France Bruno Dumont made *P'tit Quinquin*, which was shown on ARTE as well as many film festivals. Would you consider these series as a tendency of the cinematic finding its way into television? And could we thus consider a cinema education becoming part of a deeper understanding of television or moving image culture as a whole?

BERGALA: With respect to works on television I have often tried to distinguish what is *of* cinema and *of* television. A cinematic work shown on television remains a work of cinema. Some television programs, produced both for and by television, are nevertheless *of* cinema. To my mind, some of the great television series such as *The Sopranos* or *Game of Thrones* are fully-fledged works of cinema. It is neither the medium of distribution (a television screen or a cinema) nor the production context (for television or for the cinema) that define whether a work is a cinematic work or television work. It is the manner in which the director has thought, written, shot and edited his work, the model inside his or her head that is cinema – which is universal and has existed for the last 120 years. I do not believe in the theory of an "expanded cinema" according to which cinema nowadays is everywhere, which is supposedly the reason why it cannot be defined anymore. I think that accepting this theory would mean to throw away any distinction between cinema as an artistic creation and all other streams of images. Cinema is a conscious act of artistic creation. It is when a filmmaker with a personal project and a singular perspective on the world transforms these into a film by the means of mise-en-scène, his aesthetic and his artistic choices. And this desire is the one at the heart of many cinephiles and spectators. Cinema is resistant because it answeres to a unique visual regime that has touched the world for 120 years and because it correlates to a psychological desire that is fundamental and persistent.

BACHMANN: In *The Cinema Hypothesis* you argue that a truly valuable confrontation with film or with art in general always needs that moment of friction, of being confronted with otherness that stands in opposition to our experiences of the everyday. What always surprised me is that while you articulated a need for children to be confronted with a wide variety of films and filmic forms, so-called experimental or avant-garde filmmaking plays almost no role for you in that context. In my own work as a film educator or that of some of my German colleagues, such as Stefanie Schlueter or Manuel Zahn, these forms have always played a decisive role – for two reasons: on the one hand, the absence of narrative in a classical sense seems to open up the perception for the aesthetic qualities of film as an art form; on the other hand, these films often take an approach to film that deviates most strongly from the images that young people are confrontend with on a daily basis. Would you agree to this? Is there a specific reason why you talk mostly about narrative cinema?

BERGALA: You are absolutely right in this regard and if I had to write *The Cinema Hypothesis* today I would not hesitate to include experimental cinema. The DVD series *L'Eden cinéma* already included some excerpts of non-narrative cinema, such as Jonas Mekas's *Walden*. It goes without saying that for children, the younger ones especially, the absence of narration is no obstacle to an interest in and pleasure of a film. Quite the opposite. They are not yet full of preconceptions about the different categories of cinema.

One of experimental cinema's pedagogical strong points is, that it first and foremost addresses the sensual, that it foregrounds forms and rhythms that are often veiled by the characters' trajectories in narrative cinema. The fact that these films are often quite short is beneficial to dealing with them in class, in the course of a short and limited interval such as a lesson. And the really young children from kindergarten are immediately affected by and enthusiastic for the forms, colours and rhythms.

BACHMANN: Two years ago, at a conference at the Austrian Film Museum, Chris Dercon – then director of the Tate Modern in London – said that cinephilia might be one of the reasons why cinema as a whole is in decline. His criticism was mainly aimed at the discourse of cinephiles that would not take into account all those that have not yet found their love for cinema and are thus not so deeply involved in it. At the same time, people like Serge Daney have stressed time and again that writing on film is also always an act of teaching film, of providing an entry to cinema and its potentials. What is your oppinion on this and how would you articulate the role of film education in times when cinema as a whole is losing more of its role as part of an everyday culture?

BERGALA: I am currently not very optimistic when it comes to the power relations between culture and consumption. Economical ultra-liberalism prefers "customers" who are ready to "swallow" any given commodity placed in front of them and forget about it as quickly as possible so that they can consume yet another one on the next day.

Reflection and culture cannot exist without the awareness and memory of an art. These are dimensions that are in danger today. Amnesia is rapidly gaining ground even in universities and specialized cinema schools such as the one I am teaching at.

I am convinved that to talk about films, to write about cinema and to teach are the last and only forms of resistance, more essential than ever. I am saying this despite my daily experience of seeing a decline in interest to know the essential works and the history of an art form due to the accelaration of consumption that has no need for an awareness of the past. But the most fatal attitude would be to put our heads into the sand and to renounce all efforts. Experience has shown that young people's contact with works of art can be enthusiastic and profitable. It is the conditions of these encounters that we have to preserve from that ultra-liberal amnesia which makes its profit from oblivion.

BACHMANN: I feel the same way. The role of a *passeur* and of certain cinema institutions becomes more and more relevant in our current situation. But there is one point I would like to return to: Could it be that those who love cinema, write about cinema, teach cinema need to find a language, a certain discourse, an angle that always also includes or adresses those people that are not already in love with cinema? I think what Dercon was referring to and criticising was a cinephile discourse that was content to talk to those who had already found their passion for cinema and never tried to convince "all the others"?

BERGALA: The love for cinema can be very elitist indeed. Such is the case in micro-communities of cinephiles where one tends to talk about cinema only to those who already share the passion for cinema and the same films. Cinephilia sometimes is this "oratory" for those in the know, who are envious with their treasures. But those whom I would call *passeurs* have always had a passion to share their taste and the films they loved. André Bazin travelled across France after the war to share his passion for films with intellectuals at universities as well with the workers in factories. Serge Daney tried to convince all those whom he met that films could help to understand our era and our place within it. Jean Douchet, despite being a "historic cinephile"

from the Nouvelle Vague, is still motivating Ciné-clubs to show films at the Cinémathèque and elsewhere. I have personally never stopped to go to cinemas in the countryside or other countries to show films that I deem worthy of being defended – even if they are regarded as "difficult" such as works by Jean-Luc Godard or Manoel de Oliveira. And I believe that one can speak in simple terms about complex things and thus hand on powerful ideas about cinema to an unspecialized audience. At least I have always tried to do that and refrained from an academic language which tends to include only a "happy few."

FilmmuseumSynemaPublications

Available English Language Titles

Volume 26
**JEAN-MARIE STRAUB &
DANIÈLE HUILLET**
Edited by Ted Fendt
Vienna 2016, 256 pages
ISBN 978-3-901644-64-1
Jean-Marie Straub and Danièle
Huillet have distinguished themselves as two of Europe's most
inventive, generous and uncompromising filmmakers. In classics
such as *Not Reconciled, Chronicle of Anna Magdalena Bach,
Moses and Aaron, Class Relations, Antigone,* and *Sicilia!,* they
developed unique approaches to film adaptation, perform-
ance, sound recording, cinematography, and translation,
working throughout Germany, Italy and France since the
early 1960s. This book is the first English-language "primer"
on Straub and Huillet and has been published on the occasion of an extensive touring retrospective of their work in
North America and Europe. It features original essays by
Claudia Pummer, John Gianvito, Harun Farocki, Jean-Pierre
Gorin, Ted Fendt, and Barbara Ulrich, as well as François
Albera's career-spanning interview with the two filmmakers. Tracing the history of their films, their aesthetics, and
their working methods, the book places special emphasis
on the presence of Straub and Huillet in the English-
language world and includes a rich array of previously
unpublished documents and illustrations.
*"A must for anyone with an interest for intellectual and
experimental art film."* (epd film)

Volume 24
**BE SAND, NOT OIL
THE LIFE AND WORK OF
AMOS VOGEL**
Edited by Paul Cronin
Vienna 2014, 272 pages
ISBN 978-3-901644-59-7
An émigré from Austria who
arrived in New York just before
the Second World War, Amos
Vogel was one of America's
most innovative film historians and curators. In 1947 he
created *Cinema 16,* a pioneering film club aimed at audi-
ences thirsty for work "that cannot be seen elsewhere,"

and in 1963 was instrumental in establishing the New York
Film Festival. In 1974 he published the culmination of his
thoughts, the book *Film as a Subversive Art.* In the words
of Martin Scorsese: "The man was a giant." This is the first
book about Vogel.
*"An indispensable study. If the book is invaluable for gather-
ing together numerous never-before-collected or previously
unpublished pieces by Vogel himself, the newly commissioned
essays by various scholars are every bit as welcome."*
(Film Comment)

Volume 23
HOU HSIAO-HSIEN
Edited by Richard I. Suchenski
Vienna 2014, 272 pages
ISBN 978-3-901644-55-0
Hou Hsiao-hsien is the most
important figure in Taiwanese
cinema, and his sensuous, richly
nuanced films reflect everything
that is vigorous and genuine
in contemporary film culture.
Through its stylistic originality and historical gravity, Hou's
body of work opens up new possibilities for the medium.
This volume includes contributions by Olivier Assayas,
Peggy Chiao, Jean-Michel Frodon, Shigehiko Hasumi,
Jia Zhang-ke, James Quandt, and many others as well as
conversations with Hou Hsiao-hsien and some of his most
important collaborators over the decades.
*"Delicious is a good word for this book, an absolute necessity
for every serious cinephile."* (David Bordwell)

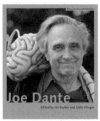

Volume 19
JOE DANTE
*Edited by Nil Baskar and
Gabe Klinger*
Vienna 2013, 256 pages
ISBN 978-3-901644-52-8
In the often dreary landscape of
Hollywood's blockbuster era,
the cinema of Joe Dante has
always stood out as a rare bea-
con of fearless originality. Blend-
ing humor with terror and trenchant political satire with
sincere tributes to "B" movies, the "Dante touch" is best

described as a mischievous free-for-all of American pop culture and film history. This first English language book on Dante includes a career-encompassing interview, a treasure trove of never-before-seen documents and illustrations, and new essays by Michael Almereyda, J. Hoberman, Bill Krohn, John Sayles, and Mark Cotta Vaz, among many others.
"The closest we currently have to a full-blown autobiography, the book does an admirable job as a single-volume overview." (Sight & Sound)

Volume 17
A POST-MAY ADOLESCENCE
LETTER TO ALICE DEBORD
By Olivier Assayas
Vienna 2012, 104 pages
ISBN 978-3-901644-44-3
Olivier Assayas is best known as a filmmaker, but cinema makes only a late appearance in his book. This reflective memoir takes us from the massive cultural upheaval that was May 1968 in France to the mid-1990s when Assayas made his first film about his teenage years. The book also includes two essays on the aesthetic and political legacy of Guy Debord, who played a decisive role in shaping the author's understanding of the world.
"Assayas' voice is clear, urgent, and persuasive. For him the matter at hand, the subject that keeps slipping away, is the story of how he came to know the work of Guy Debord. This is nothing less than the story of his life." (Film Quarterly)

Volume 16
OLIVIER ASSAYAS
Edited by Kent Jones
Vienna 2012, 256 pages
ISBN 978-3-901644-43-6
Over the past few decades, French filmmaker Olivier Assayas has become a powerful force in contemporary cinema. Between such major works as *Irma Vep, Les Destinées, Summer Hours, Carlos* and *Clouds of Sils Maria*, he has charted an exciting path, strongly embracing narrative and character and simultaneously dealing with the 'fragmentary reality' of life in a global economy. This richly-illustrated monograph includes a major essay by Kent Jones, contributions from Assayas and his most important collaborators, as well as 16 individual essays on each of the filmmaker's works.

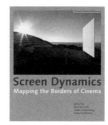

Volume 15
SCREEN DYNAMICS
MAPPING THE BORDERS OF CINEMA
Edited by Gertrud Koch, Volker Pantenburg, and Simon Rothöhler
Vienna 2012, 184 pages
ISBN 978-3-901644-39-9
This volume attempts to reconsider the limits and specifics of film and the traditional movie theater. It analyzes notions of spectatorship, the relationship between cinema and the "uncinematic", the contested place of installation art in the history of experimental cinema, and the characteristics of the high definition image. Contributors include Raymond Bellour, Victor Burgin, Vinzenz Hediger, Tom Gunning, Ute Holl, Ekkehard Knörer, Thomas Morsch, Jonathan Rosenbaum and the editors.

Volume 11
GUSTAV DEUTSCH
Edited by Wilbirg Brainin-Donnenberg and Michael Loebenstein
Vienna 2009, 252 pages
ISBN 978-3-901644-30-6
According to Viennese filmmaker Gustav Deutsch, "film is more than film." His own career proves that point. In addition to being an internationally acclaimed creator of found footage films, he is also a visual artist, an architect, a researcher, an educator, an archaeologist, and a traveler. This volume traces the way in which the cinema of Gustav Deutsch transcends our common notion of film. Essays by Nico de Klerk, Stefan Grissemann, Tom Gunning, Beate Hofstadler, Alexander Horwath, Wolfgang Kos, Scott MacDonald, Burkhard Stangl, and the editors.

Volume 9
FILM CURATORSHIP
ARCHIVES, MUSEUMS, AND
THE DIGITAL MARKETPLACE
By Paolo Cherchi Usai, David
Francis, Alexander Horwath,
and Michael Loebenstein
Vienna 2008, 240 pages
ISBN 978-3-901644-24-5
This volume deals with the
rarely-discussed discipline of
film curatorship and with the major issues and challenges
that film museums and cinémathèques are bound to face
in the Digital Age. *Film Curatorship* is an experiment: a
collective text, a montage of dialogues, conversations, and
exchanges among four professionals representing three
generations of film archivists and curators.

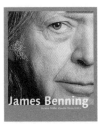

Volume 6
JAMES BENNING
Edited by Barbara Pichler
and Claudia Slanar
Vienna 2007, 264 pages
ISBN 978-3-901644-23-8
James Benning's films are
among the most fascinating
works in American cinema.
He explores the relationship
between image, text and sound
while paying expansive attention to the "vernacular landscapes" of American life. This volume traces Benning's
artistic career as well as his biographical journey through
the United States. With contributions by James Benning,
Sharon Lockhart, Allan Sekula, Dick Hebdige, Scott Mac-
Donald, Volker Pantenburg, Nils Plath, Michael Pisaro,
Amanda Yates, Sadie Benning, Julie Ault, Claudia Slanar
and Barbara Pichler.

Volume 5
JOSEF VON STERNBERG
THE CASE OF LENA SMITH
Edited by Alexander Horwath
and Michael Omasta
Vienna 2007, 304 pages
ISBN 978-3-901644-22-1
The Case of Lena Smith, directed
by Josef von Sternberg, is one of
the legendary lost masterpieces
of the American cinema. Assem-
bling 150 original stills and set designs, numerous script and
production documents as well as essays by eminent film
historians, the book reconstructs Sternberg's dramatic film
about a young woman fighting the oppressive class system
of Imperial Vienna. The book includes essays by Janet
Bergstrom, Gero Gandert, Franz Grafl, Alexander Horwath,
Hiroshi Komatsu and Michael Omasta, a preface by Meri
von Sternberg, as well as contemporary reviews and excerpts from Viennese literature of the era.

Volume 4
DZIGA VERTOV
DIE VERTOV-SAMMLUNG IM
ÖSTERREICHISCHEN FILMMUSEUM
THE VERTOV COLLECTION
AT THE AUSTRIAN FILM MUSEUM
Edited by the Austrian Film
Museum, Thomas Tode,
and Barbara Wurm
Vienna 2006, 288 pages
ISBN 3-901644-19-9
For the Russian filmmaker and film theorist Dziga Vertov
KINO was both a bold aesthetic experiment and a docu-
ment of contemporary life. This book presents the Austrian
Film Museum's comprehensive Vertov Collection, including
many unpublished documents and writings such as his
extensive autobiographical "Calling Card" from 1947.

All FilmmuseumSynemaPublications are distributed internationally by Columbia University Press (**cup.columbia.edu**).
In the German-language area please also see **www.filmmuseum.at**.